Praise for *The Joy of Being Mom*

Using her signature style of wit, wisdom, and candor, Judy gets to the heart of motherhood and uncovers practical and spiritual truths that will change your life forever. You will see yourself in many of her stories that highlight the ups and downs of being a mom. Only someone who has diligently sought and applied wisdom from God could write a book like this. *The Joy of Being Mom* will be a treasured gift for moms everywhere.

Thomas and Mary Beth Miller
Executive Strategy Pastor & Kids Pastor, Gateway Church

Judy Brisky is such a relatable mother and a fantastic writer. In this book she opens her heart and shares both the trying challenges and the soul-stirring highlights of motherhood. We believe moms from all walks of life will be blessed and encouraged, and we highly recommend *The Joy of Being Mom*.

Jimmy and Karen Evans
Elder, Gateway Church Co-founders of MarriageToday

Judy is a woman of great humility, integrity, and wisdom. She is a wonderful example of a mom who seeks the Lord in every part of her life. *The Joy of Being Mom* is full of godly insight and time-tested advice, and we are honored to give it our highest recommendation.

Mark and Jodie Harris
Worship Pastor, Gateway Church

This book is a refreshing and honest look at motherhood. Judy tells her own story with such transparency and encouragement. The Study Guide questions and activities provide an excellent opportunity to reflect on and personalize the truths in each chapter. This is a book that will impact any mother in a profound way.

Cassie Reid, Ph Supervisor
Director of Marriage and Fa— University
Ow ounseling

We have known and loved Judy 20 years.
We have watched them parent principles

and train them in the way they should go. We also had the honor of walking closely with them during the short but precious life of their daughter, Dani. Judy does more than teach principles of godly parenting—she lives them! We highly recommend this book to every woman who wants a mentor to walk with on the journey of motherhood.

Steve and Melody Dulin
Founding Elder and Apostolic Pastor, Gateway Church

FOREWORD BY ROBERT AND DEBBIE MORRIS

JUDY BRISKY

THE JOY OF BEING MOM

Embrace the Adventure

WITH STUDY GUIDE

DEDICATION

First and foremost, this book is dedicated to my Lord and Savior, Jesus Christ. When You opened my eyes to Your truth, You also opened my heart to being a mom. I am eternally grateful for both. You hold my heart, my life, and my family. I love You, Jesus.

Second, this book is dedicated to my husband, Michael. I am so thankful that the Lord brought you into my life and that we came to salvation through Jesus. Together, we've come to know the love of God in greater measure as we seek to live in the power of the Holy Spirit every day. Michael, you have always believed in me, and your encouragement is such a gift to my heart. The best is yet to come, my love. Thirty years and counting! I love you.

Third, this book is dedicated to our children:

    Jacob and his wife, Neeli, and their baby in heaven, Poppy

    Joel and his wife, Danielle (Danny)

And our children in heaven:

    Our first baby

    Our son, Jared

    Our daughter, Michaela Danielle (Dani)

You are the reasons I have the blessing of being Mom! I've had my shortcomings along the way, but you have graciously loved me through them. It is because of you that I have grown to have a deeper understanding of God's love for me. I am forever grateful, and I love you, Jesus!

TABLE OF CONTENTS

FOREWORD

While we often say the best part of having kids is having grandkids, the truth is family is, and always has been, very important to us. When we started having children more than three decades ago, we were young, naïve, and not fully prepared, yet we recognized that God entrusted to us as parents the responsibility of instructing and stewarding our children in His ways. We raised each of them with the Bible as our guide, instilling solid Christian values. By the grace of God, today all three of our amazing children and their wonderful spouses are serving the Lord together in ministry.

Even so, parenting wasn't always easy. If we'd only had a book like this to help us navigate and better understand how to parent God's way. That's why we were so excited when we found out our dear friend, Judy, was writing this book. We knew it would be full of wisdom and truth about motherhood.

Judy and her husband, Mike, have been close friends of ours for more than 20 years. Before we ever met, a mutual friend told me (Robert) about a young Christian man who was playing on the PGA tour. As he was sharing, God put a burden on my heart to pray for him and his family. I started keeping up with him and watching him on TV, and a year later the opportunity arose for us to meet. We made an instant connection, and a lasting friendship began. It was during our first meeting that the Lord gave me a word for both him and Judy. It was exactly what they had been praying about as a couple and served as a confirmation from the Lord.

Over the years, we've grown closer as friends. We've walked with them through good times—watching their boys grow up and go on to get married to wonderful Christian women—as well as hard times, including the deaths of their son and newborn daughter. We've also watched Judy become one of the best mothers we've ever seen!

Judy prayerfully seeks God first in everything she does and has lived out the principles found in this book. She's mentored hundreds of young mothers over the years and taught the principles found in this book in small groups. When we think of Judy, the verses in Proverbs 31:26–29 come to mind:

> She opens her mouth with wisdom,
> And on her tongue *is* the law of kindness.
> She watches over the ways of her household,
> And does not eat the bread of idleness.
> Her children rise up and call her blessed;
> Her husband *also,* and he praises her:
> "Many daughters have done well,
> But you excel them all" (NKJV).

We know if you ever met Judy, you'd feel the same way.

We love how Judy writes to moms of all ages and stages of life. She shows how to have joy in all situations by giving an honest, front-row seat to her own personal journey as a mom—with all the victories and struggles. Rooted in God's Word, this book will inspire and encourage you to find the joy in being a mom as you embrace the adventure. It will help you overcome any shortcomings you may have and is sure to be a blessing to you.

Robert and Debbie Morris
Senior Pastor of Gateway Church
Bestselling Author of *The Blessed Life, Beyond Blessed,*
and *Take the Day Off*

ACKNOWLEDGMENTS

Thank you, Pastor Robert and Debbie Morris, for your godly example of humility and obedience to God's Word. Mike and I have been blessed by your ministry for more than 20 years, and our lives have been forever impacted by your friendship and encouragement. Thank you for your leadership in the body of Christ.

Thank you, Gateway Publishing, for walking with me on this amazing journey. Your team is incredibly talented, and your passion for the Kingdom of God is evident in all you do.

- To Craig Dunnagan and John Andersen: Thank you for your encouragement and for the opportunity to make this dream of mine a reality.
- To Jenny Morgan: Thank you for hearing my heart and knowing my voice as you thoughtfully and meticulously edited my manuscript.
- To Kathy Krenzien: Thank you for always being available to answer questions and for making the writing process easy and enjoyable.
- To Peyton Sepeda and Jeremy Willis: Thank you for carrying my book across the finish line and getting it into the hands of moms who need to know the love of Jesus.

A special thank you to Danielle Brisky, my daughter-in-love. Danny, your artistic talent is a beautiful and fun addition to the book! Each coloring page that you drew serves as a reminder of God's beauty and creativity. I'm thankful for you and your gifting!

INTRODUCTION

Be on guard. Stand firm in the faith. Be courageous. Be strong. And do everything with love.

—1 Corinthians 16:13–14

Dear Lord,

I'm falling apart. The boys were having a hard time sleeping last night, and I thought I was going to go crazy. Really! I lose my temper all the time with the slightest thing. I'm always yelling, always raising my voice. I don't want to be like that. I don't want my kids to remember their mother as someone who was always angry, always yelling. I don't know what to do. Potty training? Ha! Jacob couldn't care less, and I don't have the umph! to get things going. What a mess I've made of my family. I'm so overwhelmed with so much to do at home. When am I supposed to clean with two little ones at my feet? Please help me. I feel so out of control. I want the house to look nice and clean. I want to feel better organized about my family. I want to be more loving. Please, please help me.

(A tough day in 1997)

What exhausted, frazzled mom wrote this journal entry? I have to confess—it was me. Your next thought may be, *How could the same woman possibly write a book about motherhood and joy?* Well, first let me assure you that I did eventually potty train Jacob, as well as his brother, Joel. And there were even bigger changes:

- I learned to stop yelling.
- I discovered the importance of teaching and training.
- I stopped feeling overwhelmed all the time.
- I learned to trust the Lord and not worry about every little thing.

Keeping the house organized and clean became something I absolutely love. Yes, really. (Except for toilets—those are still not my favorite). My home looks nice and tidy more often than not.

And if you ask my family, they will tell you that my prayer to become more loving was answered too. I am incredibly blessed and grateful to be married to my husband, Michael (Mike). We are 30 years strong! Our sons, Jacob and Joel, are now grown and married, and I love the close relationships I have with them and my daughters-in-love, Neeli and Danny. I also have such a great relationship with my dad, and he lives with Michael and me.

How did I turn things around? How did I go from being a loud and crazy mom to a not-so-loud but way more fun mom? The answer is simple—I prayed and asked God to help me. I read His Word. And once I started doing those things, I didn't stop. I made God the center of my life, my marriage, and my parenting.

I didn't write this book with the notion that I am an "expert" mom. I'll be the first to admit I haven't done everything right. God has done amazing things in my life *despite my shortcomings*, and I believe He can and will do the same for you if you allow Him into your world. He brings healing, love, and restoration to every person who seeks Him and follows His ways.

This book is meant to serve as a launching pad as you seek God's heart. Some of the ideas and activities that worked well for my family may be a great match for you, and other things may need some adjustment or fine-tuning. The important thing is that you seek the Lord through prayer and His Word for what He wants for you and your family.

Each chapter includes a coloring page with an encouraging Scripture. At the end of each chapter is a study guide with Scriptures, questions (which are great for personal reflection or group study), and activities called "Heart Connectors" to help you grow in your relationship with God and your family.

As you read, I encourage you to keep a journal nearby to write your thoughts, prayers, and anything else the Lord puts on your heart. You see, once you start reading the Bible and making prayer a part of your day, you'll begin to understand God's heart for you in every area of your life.

When I talk about different parenting topics, you'll find that I use the word "children" in regard to anything that covers the family. There are certain topics where I will give some estimated ages; however, these are not hard or fast rules. Some children mature earlier, while others mature later. Any given age distinctions may or may not fit your children's developmental stages when you read this book. I encourage you to be prayerful as only you (and your spouse, if married) can determine what works best for your family.

I pray this book will encourage you as a woman, a wife, a mom, and a daughter of the King. The Lord loves you so much, and He has wonderful plans for you on this journey called motherhood.

Father God, You are so good. Your love for us is beyond measure. Please open our hearts to receive anything You want to give us. Thank You for our sweet families. May our love for each other reflect Your love for us. In Jesus' name, Amen.

CHAPTER 1

IS THIS ALL THERE IS?

God is so rich in mercy, and he loved us so much, that even though we were dead because of our sins, he gave us life when he raised Christ from the dead. (It is only by God's grace that you have been saved!)

—Ephesians 2:4–5

On April 21, 1990, I married my sweetheart, Mike, in my hometown in South Texas. One week later, we moved to Orlando, Florida. (We chose Florida because it is a good place to live if you're a professional golfer, which Mike was at the time.) I had always lived in Texas until then, but the transition was fairly easy for me. Soon, I was working full-time, Mike was playing weekly golf tournaments, and we were attending a nearby church. We were doing well. Yes, we had some struggles during that early married season, but overall, things were good—until one rainy Sunday morning.

It was just over a year into our marriage, and we were getting ready to attend church services. Out of nowhere, Mike brought up something that had been an on-again, off-again topic of conversation over the course of our five-year relationship (four years dating and one year married). He said, "What is life really all about? We eat. We work. We sleep. Then we do it all over again. What for? What's the point? I mean, is this really all there is?" I wish I could tell you that I immediately came to his side, affirmed my love for him, and told him I understood his confusion. But the truth is I was hurt. His apparent anguish over life's meaning caught me off guard, and I felt it was my fault. I asked, "Is it me? Am I the reason you're feeling so confused about life?" Immediately, Mike answered, "No, it has nothing to do with you." I should have been relieved, but I wasn't. Instead, I felt left out.

We continued the conversation, both of us in tears. Yes, we loved each other. Yes, we were committed to each other. But what about life in general? Why were we here? What was our purpose? As we continued to talk things through, I asked Mike, "Why don't we read the Bible?" Then I silently wondered, *Where did that idea come from?* Yes, we attended church, but reading the Bible was not a normal part of our lives. (I realize now that it was the Holy Spirit speaking to my heart.)

I found a Bible tucked away in our bedroom closet. We were hoping to find the answers to life's deepest questions, but we didn't know where to start reading. I opened the Bible and found a page that said something to the effect of, "If you've never read the Bible, start with the book of John." But where was the book of John? I looked at the glossary and found the page number for "John." I read the first verse:

> In the beginning the Word already existed.
> > The Word was with God,
> > and the Word was God (John 1:1).

It was beautiful and amazing and comforting. Mike and I cried as I continued reading, and we decided we would read the Bible every day.

Several weeks later, Mike began traveling again to play some golf tournaments. He had met another golfer, Ralph, who was set to play in the same tournaments. To help with travel expenses, they decided to be roommates on the road. I didn't know much about Ralph, and I wasn't completely comfortable with Mike traveling with a guy we hardly knew. Still, I trusted my husband's decision. Mike wanted to keep reading the Bible while he was away, but he didn't have his own copy. I told him that most hotel rooms have a Bible he could read, but he was uncomfortable doing that in front of Ralph. Mike asked, "What would Ralph think? Would he think it's weird for me to be reading a hotel Bible? Or weird to be reading a Bible at all?" We decided that the best solution was for me to read the Bible to him over the phone every night.

There was just one flaw in our plan—long-distance calls weren't cheap. We soon realized that our nightly phone routine of catching up and me reading Scripture was getting expensive. Mike needed to get his own Bible so he could read it in the hotel room. He also decided to be upfront with Ralph and asked if he believed in Jesus. That conversation was the beginning of the most important time in our lives! As it turned out, Ralph was a Christian. He was even planning to lead a Bible study on the golf tour they were playing on that year. I couldn't believe it! God had arranged for Mike and Ralph to meet, quickly become friends, and be roommates on the tour so that my husband could be mentored by someone who loved the Lord and His Word.

SALVATION

Ralph took Mike to a Christian bookstore and helped him pick out a Bible. A few months later, I visited my husband in Cary, North Carolina, and we attended Ralph's Bible study. Now, Mike and I loved the Lord, and we had been diligently reading our Bibles. However, that meeting was the first time we heard about *salvation* (which is also called "being born again"). Growing up, I believed that if I was a good person, then

I would go to heaven after I died. Of course, "good" is a relative term, but I tried to do more good things than bad things. Sitting in that Bible study, though, Mike and I realized that salvation wasn't about being good.

We also learned that there is an enemy who wants to keep us from following God. This enemy is the devil, and his goal is to make us believe that our sins are too terrible to be forgiven. You see, it is true that sin separates us from God. He is perfect and holy, and anything that is not perfect and holy cannot enter His presence. You and I can never be good enough to earn our way into heaven. But the devil doesn't want anyone to know that God Himself provided the solution.

> For this is how God loved the world: He gave his one and only Son, so that everyone who believes in him will not perish but have eternal life (John 3:16).

You may be thinking, *Why would God do that for me?* The answer is simple: God made you, and He loves you. The number one desire of God's heart is to have a relationship with you. That is why He sent His Son, Jesus Christ, to die on the cross and pay the price for the sins of all humanity.

The number one desire of God's heart is to have a relationship with you.

And there's more! Not only did Jesus conquer sin, but He also conquered death. Through God's resurrection power, Jesus rose again three days later. This same power is available to us when we surrender our lives and accept Jesus as our Savior.

We are made right with God by placing our faith in Jesus Christ. And this is true for everyone who believes, no matter who we are.

> For everyone has sinned; we all fall short of God's glorious standard. Yet God, in his grace, freely makes us right in his sight. He did this through Christ Jesus when he freed us from the penalty for our sins. For God presented Jesus as the sacrifice for sin. People are made right with God when they believe that Jesus sacrificed his life, shedding his blood (Romans 3:22–25).

> God saved you by his grace when you believed. And you can't take credit for this; it is a gift from God. Salvation is not a reward for the good things we have done, so none of us can boast about it (Ephesians 2:8–9).

> He [Jesus] was handed over to die because of our sins, and he was raised to life to make us right with God (Romans 4:25).

Mike and I had found the answer to that nagging question, "What is life really all about?" For the first time, everything made sense! We knew we needed to stop trying to live by our own strength and surrender our lives to Jesus Christ.

Is something stirring inside your heart right now? Maybe you have tried to be a "good" person but still feel as though something is lacking. Or perhaps you have really struggled in some areas and feel hopelessly unlovable. Sweet friend, God is so gracious. He will meet you right where you are if you just call out to Him. You can use your own words, or you are welcome to pray as Mike and I did:

Dear God,
I admit that I am a sinner. Today, I surrender my life to You.
I believe that You sent Your Son, Jesus, to die on the cross for

my sins and that He rose again on the third day. Jesus, I ask
You to be my Lord and Savior. Thank You that I am comple-
tely forgiven and accepted into Your family. I choose to live
for You from this day forward. In Jesus' name, Amen.

If you prayed that prayer, let me be the first to say, "Welcome to the family of God!" This is the best decision you will ever make. God is your heavenly Father, and He will never leave you. The blood of Jesus covers every single sin you have ever committed or ever will commit. Now, there may be lingering consequences for choices you've made in the past, and you may have to address some painful circumstances or broken relationships. But God will be with you every step of the way. He will give you wisdom and strength as you move forward and live for Him.

WATER BAPTISM

After accepting Jesus as your Lord and Savior, the first step in your new life as a Christian is water baptism. If you are unfamiliar with water baptism, I highly encourage you to read about it in the New Testament. Water baptism serves as an outward sign of what God has done in your heart and in your life. Being immersed in water during baptism symbolizes Christ's burial after His death on the cross, and coming out of the water represents new life in Christ just as He was raised to life again.

Here is what the apostle Paul wrote about water baptism:

For we died and were buried with Christ by baptism. And just as Christ was raised from the dead by the glorious power of the Father, now we also may live new lives (Romans 6:4).

IS THIS ALL THERE IS?

Water baptism is an act of faith and obedience. Jesus set the example for us when He, in obedience to God, was baptized (see Matthew 3:13–17).

Water baptism doesn't have to take place in a church building. All you need is some water and another believer to baptize you. Mike and I didn't want to wait until we got home from North Carolina, so with a group of friends cheering us on, we were baptized in a hotel swimming pool. It was great!

QUIET TIMES

When Mike and I became Christians, we learned about the importance of spending time with God every day. We made it a priority to pray and read God's Word every day. These special times with the Lord are often called "quiet times."

Some people feel as if they have to follow strict quiet time rules—they have to pray for a specific amount of time, read a certain number of chapters in their Bible, etc. If they fail to meet this quota, or even worse, miss a day, then they mentally beat themselves up. Now, I am not a pastor or a theologian, but I have been a Christian for almost 30 years. I have discovered that there is no one-size-fits-all "right" way to have a quiet time. God made all of us wonderfully unique, which means each person's relationship with Him is going to be unique too.

I have also found that quiet times tend to change during the different seasons of life. If you are a mom with young children, your times with God may not be so "quiet." That is okay! God cares much more about your heart than the noise level in the room. Ask Him to help you find creative ways to spend time with Him while taking care of your family. The more time you spend in God's presence, the more His peace will fill your heart and mind.

> The more time you spend in God's presence, the more His peace will fill your heart and mind.

THE BIBLE

The Bible is the most important book you will ever read. Many people call it "God's love letter" because from beginning to end, it speaks of His great love for us.

> You made all the delicate, inner parts of my body
> and knit me together in my mother's womb.
> Thank you for making me so wonderfully complex!
> Your workmanship is marvelous—how well I know it.
> You watched me as I was being formed in utter seclusion,
> as I was woven together in the dark of the womb.
> You saw me before I was born.
> Every day of my life was recorded in your book.
> Every moment was laid out
> before a single day had passed.
> How precious are your thoughts about me, O God.
> They cannot be numbered!
> I can't even count them;
> they outnumber the grains of sand!
> And when I wake up,
> you are still with me! (Psalm 139:13–18).

God's thoughts about you are precious, and "they outnumber the grains of sand." That's a lot of sweet thoughts your Father has for you!

Any time you read the Bible, begin by asking God to guide you and help you understand as you read. It may seem like there's too much to learn, but He will help you. God's Word will bring you encouragement when you need it and direction when you're unsure of what to do. It will help you in your toughest moments and bring reassurance as you grow in your relationship with the Lord.

FELLOWSHIP

God designed us to be *relational*. In other words, we are not meant to do life alone. As a Christian, it is important to build relationships with other believers who will encourage you to grow in your faith. The best way to start is by joining a Bible-believing church where the Word of God is preached and followed. Many churches offer classes or small groups, and these are great opportunities to get to know people who share your love for the Lord.

WHAT DOES ALL THIS HAVE TO DO WITH BEING A MOM?

Why did I begin a book about motherhood with my story of salvation and some key aspects of living as a Christian? Because I believe that having a relationship with God is the essential foundation for life.

The most important part of a house is the foundation. If the foundation is properly laid, then the house will remain level and secure. However, if there are problems with the foundation, then there will be problems with the house too. The damage from storms will be more severe, and the cost to repair such damage will also be greater.

The same is true for our lives. We need to be planted in the strong spiritual foundation that is found in Jesus Christ. Being a Christian does not mean difficult events or painful situations will never happen again. We still live in a broken world. But our relationship with God gives us hope and strength in every circumstance and battle.

When the storms of life come, the wicked are whirled away,
but the godly have a lasting foundation (Proverbs 10:25).

When we invite God into our lives, He lays the foundation and begins to remodel our hearts. He removes the things that would keep us from living the life He has planned for us. There may be bad habits that need to be broken, fractured relationships that need mending, or unhealthy choices that need to be addressed. The remodeling process may not be comfortable, and at times you may wonder, *Is it worth it?* I promise it is. God loves you so much, and He wants you to live a healthy, joy-filled life. His plans for you are good. You can trust Him.

CHAPTER 1

STUDY GUIDE

REVIEW

A relationship with God is the essential foundation for life. When you accept Jesus Christ as your Lord and Savior, you receive complete forgiveness for your sins and the power to live as a child of God. Water baptism is an outward act of obedience that signifies the change inside your heart. It is important to build your faith by spending time with God, reading His Word, and developing relationships with other believers.

SCRIPTURES

- Romans 3:22–28
- Romans 5:6–11
- Ephesians 1:3–8
- Ephesians 2:1–10

QUESTIONS

- Many people wonder, *What is the purpose of life*? How would you answer that question?
- What are some ways you can spend time with God in your current season of life?
- Why is it so important to have close relationships with other believers?

HEART CONNECTORS

- Write a "Thank You" note to God. Tell Him what He means to you and how grateful you are to be His child. Keep the note in your Bible or journal. It will serve as a reminder to you of how you felt when you first accepted Jesus as your Lord and Savior.

- Set aside some one-on-one time with each of your children and share your salvation story with them. Allow your child to ask questions and invite him or her to continue asking questions at any time. Finally, record the conversation in your journal so that you will have a sweet remembrance of your talk.

PRAYER

Father God, You are so good to me. Thank You for sending Your Son, Jesus, to pay the price for my sins and set me free. Your love amazes me! Thank You for Your Word and Your presence. Please show me anything in my heart that displeases You and help me be the mom You have called me to be. May my life bring You glory, honor, and praise. In Jesus' name, Amen.

CHAPTER 2

ALL MY CHILDREN

He gives the childless woman a family,
*   making her a happy mother.*
Praise the LORD!

—Psalm 113:9

When Mike and I got married, it was understood that we weren't going to have children. Don't get me wrong—I loved children. I just didn't want to have any of my own. Truth be told, I was scared to be a mom. What if my children got made fun of, bullied, or hurt in some way? What if I couldn't protect them? I honestly didn't think my heart could handle that.

After I accepted Jesus as the Lord of my life, one of the first things that changed was my desire to be a mom. I discussed it with Mike, and he told me he knew all along that we would one day be parents. What? He knew it all along? "Yes," he said, "I figured you'd eventually change your mind." And he was right!

OUR FIRST BABY

A few years later, I became pregnant. We were overwhelmed with joy and gratitude. I was working full-time, but we decided that I would stay at home once our baby was born. Almost 10 weeks into my pregnancy, I noticed some bleeding. We immediately went to see my doctor and received the heartbreaking news that I had had a miscarriage. We had lost our first baby. I was shocked, confused, and sad.

Mike stayed home for several weeks while I was recovering, but then he had to start traveling again for work. One night while he was away, I felt overcome by the pain and grief of our loss. I asked the Lord for a verse that would encourage me and help me sleep. Immediately, I saw "Psalm 4:8" in my mind. I opened my Bible and read:

> In peace I will lie down and sleep,
>> for you alone, LORD,
>> make me dwell in safety (Psalm 4:8 NIV).

The Lord gave me just what I needed in that moment. That verse got me through a lot of sleepless nights.

JACOB

With lots of prayer and support, our hearts recovered, and five months later we found ourselves pregnant again. I was thrilled! I didn't care that I was often nauseated or that I threw up every morning or that I was sleepy all the time. I was going to have a baby, and that was all that mattered! I wrote a letter to God in my journal.

> *Heavenly Father,*
> *It's been almost two days since we discovered we're going to have a baby. I can't explain how I feel. I'm so happy, Father. Thank You. I kind of feel like it's a dream. Thank You, Father. There are times I feel so much joy it's unbelievable. Father, I cry as I write. How do I thank You? I love You so very much.*

Therefore I tell you, whatever you ask for in prayer, believe that you have received it, and it will be yours (Mark 11:24 NIV).

[This is] The verse You gave me in what seems like such a long time ago. Thank You, dear God, that You have blessed Michael and me in such a mighty way. I plan, with Your unending help and strength, to thoroughly enjoy this baby! You know, Father, I've had thoughts about ... What if something goes wrong? What if our baby's not healthy? Right now, in the name of Jesus, who is Lord and Savior, I rebuke those thoughts. Help me, Lord, to keep my gaze only on You. I want to follow Your plan for my life. I pray, Father, for the health of our baby. In these early stages, I pray that everything is developing healthfully. I pray this be Your will. I love You, Father. In Jesus' name, Amen!

I would love to tell you that after I prayed and wrote my letter to God, fear never entered my mind or heart again. But it did. I sometimes still had the fearful thought, *What if we lose this baby too?* "What ifs" can really make what should be a joyful experience quite stressful. I had to put my focus on the Lord and choose to believe what His Word says about faith and trust in Him. I made the decision to enjoy my pregnancy to the fullest extent and not worry about our little one.

> **I had to put my focus on the Lord and choose to believe what His Word says about faith and trust in Him.**

When I was about 20 weeks pregnant, we found out that our baby was a boy. We were so happy! I had such incredible joy, despite still feeling nauseated and despite the enemy's whispers that this baby wouldn't survive. Whenever any doubts or fears came into my mind, I immediately took them to God.

Father, I feel our baby move inside me so much these days. It's amazing. I can't believe I have a life growing inside of me. I feel overwhelmed at times. I worry about being a good mommy, I worry about knowing how to care for our baby. I guess they're normal concerns, but still, at times, I worry. Help me, Father! I want to rest in You and feel safe and secure. I love You!

Right on his due date, our son was born. He had big, dark eyes and lots of dark brown hair. Mike and I were thankful beyond words for our precious boy, and we named him Jacob.

The first few months of motherhood were a bit difficult for me. Mike was playing on the PGA Tour, and just three weeks after Jacob was born, we were all on the road. I was nervous and worried about being a mom. What if Jacob needed something and I didn't know how to help him? What if I went to the grocery store and he started crying? Once again, the "what ifs" were crowding my brain.

I finally came to the realization that no one was watching me or grading me on my mom skills. Jacob did cry at the grocery store, and guess what? We both survived. I needed to stop worrying and start enjoying being Mom to my son. It took a little while, but this new mindset helped me become more and more comfortable going out by myself with Jacob.

Jacob was a cheerful baby. Yes, he cried sometimes, but he also loved to laugh and talk! As a child, his favorite things were books. Jacob always seemed to have a book in his hands, and this habit continued into adulthood. In fact, he now makes his living as a writer. It amazes me how God designs every person with unique gifts and talents that are just right for them. He is such a good Father!

JOEL

Eighteen months after Jacob was born, Mike and I talked about how great it would be to have another baby. To our surprise, we got pregnant right away. Again, we were thrilled, but I also had some concerns. I wondered, *Will I be able to love our new baby as much as I love our son? Will Jacob feel less important now that he will have a younger sibling?* I felt guilty that Jacob wouldn't have me all to himself anymore and that our new baby would never know what it was like to have me all to himself or herself. All these things pulled on my heart.

As a Christian, I knew it was important to bring everything to the Lord in prayer. So that's what I did. Every time a worry or concern came into my mind, I brought it to God. He showed me that children are born in the perfect order. Jacob was meant to be the oldest, and not only would he still feel loved, but he would also be the perfect big brother. The Lord also assured me that this new baby wouldn't feel any less loved as the second-born child; he or she would be surrounded by love from Mike, myself, and Jacob.

Eight and a half months later, Joel was born. He arrived two weeks before his due date (the first sign of a life-long preference for being early), and like his big brother, he had brown eyes and a head full of hair. I remember Jacob walking into the hospital room to see his baby brother. He was so proud, and even though he was only 27 months old, he looked so big! I later wrote this in my journal:

Heavenly Father,

Joel is four days old today. He is such a joy! He's really beautiful! I'm so thankful that the delivery went smoothly. Only 30 minutes of pushing. Thank You, God! I'm most grateful that Joel is healthy. Thank You, Father. I still have worries, and I'm sorry. I know that worrying is not trusting You. I want to trust You, Lord.

Joel was a happy baby with lots of energy and a smile that never stopped. Mike was still playing professional golf, and we went all over the country as a family. Jacob and Joel were great travelers, and they made friends in airports, golf courses, and hotels from east to west. It was important to Mike and me that we all travel together and not be apart for long periods of time. Plus, it was fun visiting cities from coast to coast.

As the boys got older, we became a homeschooling family. One advantage to this method of education was that we could visit many of the places we read about in books. I read somewhere that camping is a good way to bring families closer and build relationships. I remember thinking, *Living in hotels just about every week is like camping—but with real bathrooms!* Our home base was still in Orlando, and it was always fun to go home, reconnect with friends, and attend our home church.

JARED

By the time Jacob was eight and Joel was six, Mike and I decided to move our family back to Texas. We made our new home in the Dallas area. I hadn't gotten pregnant since Joel was born, and I thought our family of four might be complete. Then, in the fall of 2002, we got a big surprise—we were going to have another baby! My first reaction was one of shock, followed by joy and elation. I really didn't think I would ever be pregnant again, but here we were. The nausea was intense during the first trimester, and I remember the sense of relief when it subsided. I could now enjoy the thought of having three little ones.

Our boys were excited and couldn't wait for the baby to arrive. We all started thinking of possible names. At my

20-week appointment, the doctor began his examination, but it soon became clear that he was having trouble finding the baby's heartbeat. Several long minutes passed, and the doctor proceeded to do an ultrasound. Our baby's heart had stopped beating.

I couldn't believe it. It was all so numbing. We decided to wait a couple of days to have another ultrasound in the hopes of hearing a heartbeat. However, the second ultrasound confirmed the findings of the first—we had lost our baby. Because I was so far along in my pregnancy, the doctor scheduled my delivery date.

Mike and I arrived at the hospital on a dark February night around 9 pm. I remember going to check in at the nurses' station on the maternity floor and thinking how strange it was for me to be near other moms who were getting ready to give birth to their babies. As we walked to my room, my ears filled with the expectant cries of mothers in labor and the sweet cries of newborns.

"Oh, God," I prayed silently, "please help me." My doctor was a Christian, and he gave me a paper with a Scripture verse written on it that evening. I wish I had kept it, but it got lost in the busyness of that night. Still, I remember thinking how kind it was of him to do that for us.

Once in the room, I got settled in bed, and Mike sat next to me in a reclining chair. I think it was around midnight that a nurse gave me some medication to cause my body to go into labor. I was able to sleep off and on during the night, but around 6 am I woke up and knew something was happening. There was no pain or discomfort—just a knowing. I called out to Mike, and within minutes I felt our baby slip out of my body. I then had Mike call the nurse to let her know what happened. She quickly came into the room and asked how I was feeling. She took our tiny baby's body away and returned to examine me. Then she left the room.

Our doctor was notified, and we were asked if we would like to see our baby. We said yes. He was brought to us in a small crocheted blue blanket that cradled his tiny body. Yes, "he"—we had another little boy. I have to admit that I was a little nervous about seeing him. I didn't know what he would look like. But all those apprehensions melted away when I saw my son. He was so small and not fully formed, but he was beautiful. He was our baby. We named him Jared.

We planned a memorial service, where Mike and our senior pastor spoke about our Jared. Our friends rallied around us and took such good care of our family. They provided us with meals, special gifts and outings for Jacob and Joel, and unending prayer. We were incredibly blessed by the outpouring of love we received.

DANI

Time passed, and our hearts began to heal. After months of praying, Mike decided to change careers. He had played professional golf for 15 years, and now he felt the Lord leading him into full-time ministry at our church.

In November 2003, we were adjusting to our new life when God brought another change. We were going to have a baby! I definitely did not expect to be pregnant again, but God had other plans for our family. Our baby was due around the fourth of July, and we were surprised and thrilled.

Although I didn't feel my best during the first couple of months of pregnancy, the hardest part was my mother's passing in mid-November. Helping my dad organize her funeral in South Texas was tough. Then in early January, Mike's dad suffered an aneurysm. Mike returned to South Texas to visit his father at the hospital. Weeks later, as our family was driving to see him, Dad Brisky passed away. We attended the funeral, visited with family, and returned to North Texas.

Once home, we got back to getting ready for our baby. We'd already had preliminary checkups with my doctor, and all was going well so far. Because I was older, the doctor recommended a Level 2 ultrasound with a specialist. Soon Mike, the boys, and I were sitting in the specialist's office, waiting to find out if we were having a boy or a girl.

My name was called, and I walked into the examination room to get ready for the ultrasound. Once I was lying on the bed, Mike and the boys were called to join me. The specialist placed the ultrasound wand on my stomach and began moving it around. The first thing he said was, "You are having a girl." A girl! How fun would that be? Tea parties, lots of pink, dolls ...

My joyful planning was abruptly cut short when the specialist turned to the nurse and said, "Why don't you take the boys out for a soda." I knew something must be very wrong. As soon as our sons were out of the room, the specialist pointed to the screen and said, "I see a red flag here and here and here." I thought to myself, *If there are so many red flags, then how can he possibly see my baby?* The specialist kept talking, rattling off several chromosomal issues our baby girl might have. To me, it was all a jumble of confusing words. There were only three things I understood:

1. She would likely not survive to 30 weeks inside me.
2. If she did survive to 30 weeks, she would likely not survive labor.
3. If she did survive labor, she would never leave the hospital.

"Oh God! Please help me. Please help our baby!" I cried inside my head. I honestly don't know how I kept breathing. It was a nightmare. I have no memory of getting dressed and very little recollection of getting in the elevator and walking to the parking garage. But I do remember sitting in the car and crying uncontrollably. Our boys were in the back seat, and Mike explained to them, as best he could, what had happened.

When we got home, I called my dear friend Melody. She and her daughter came to the house and prayed over me and our baby girl. They cried with me too.

Initially, I was overcome with fear and grief. It was hard to focus on life in general, but I had two young sons who needed their mom. We were still homeschooling, and I was determined to keep things as normal as I could. I even continued to serve on the worship team at our church for the next several months.

I never went back to see that specialist. I had asked him if there was anything he could do for our baby, and he said, "No." Mike and I chose to continue with my regular doctor who had always been encouraging regardless of the circumstances. Together, we all prayed and hoped for a miracle.

Before our visit to the specialist, a friend of mine who was also pregnant had asked me if I had a "word" for our baby. She told me that in each of her pregnancies, she had asked the Lord for a word for her child. I loved the idea, and I asked the Lord to give me a word for our baby. Immediately, I sensed the word "miracle." Little did I know how much I would need that word in the months to come.

My days were filled with the usual things. The boys continued their homeschooling schedule, Mike went to work, and I did all the things moms do. Every once in a while (usually at night), I cried. I would go to another room where I could be alone and cry out to God to heal our baby. I prayed so hard! There were days when I truly believed she was going to be completely healthy. There were other days when I was overwhelmed with the thought of our little girl having severe health problems.

As the months went by, I can honestly say that life became normal again (or at least mostly normal, considering our situation). I focused on God and His faithfulness. Decorating the nursery was enjoyable for me as I planned how to make it really beautiful for our little girl. We also settled on a name—Michaela Danielle. I wanted to call her Michaela after her daddy, but Mike really liked Danielle. So we decided to use both names and call her "Danielle."

The last few months before Danielle was born were filled with planning, dreaming, and praying. Between baby showers and doctor appointments, Mike and I focused on how we would take care of our baby if she was born with any medical problems. We were praying for a miracle, but we also believed it was important to be prepared. Our sons knew their baby sister might have some health issues, and we did our best to answer any questions they had.

The specialist had said Danielle probably wouldn't survive to 30 weeks inside me, but she did. In fact, she made it to the full 40 weeks! Mike and I arrived at the hospital just before 6:30 am. My friend Melody and her daughter were already there, and they had decorated my room. It was beautiful!

As the morning went by, I took medication to help begin contractions. My hope was to deliver naturally, but several hours into labor, our baby girl was in distress. The doctor said I needed a C-section. I was quickly wheeled away and prepped for surgery. I had such a peace during this time—I wasn't nervous or scared. Our Danielle had already proven to be a fighter, and we were ready to meet her. Mike soon joined me in the surgery suite. He sat right next to the operating table so that we could be face to face, and he prayed.

A curtain hung above the operating table, and I couldn't see anything below my waist. The doctor began the procedure, talking us through every step. I felt the tugging as he lifted Danielle from my body. We listened intently for her cry. There was silence for what seemed like forever, but finally, there it was. A soft, little cry. Thank You, God! Our daughter was alive, and I could hear her. Mike went to see her and came back with a smile and some tears in his eyes. He told me he could see that our baby had some problems. We cried together, and I told him, "It's okay. We're going to be okay."

Before our little girl was born, I told Mike and the boys that her name was Danielle, *not* Dani. There would be no nicknames for our girl, and that was final. But when the nurse brought her to me, the first words out of my mouth were "Hi Dani!" She really was so beautiful, with the softest little cry coming from her tiny body. Mike and I had read quite a bit about different chromosomal abnormalities and knew that even a full-term baby might be born very small. Dani came into the world weighing five pounds and two ounces.

The next few days were filled with lots of doctors, examinations, and tests for our baby. None of the reports were good. Our Dani had a chromosome 18 abnormality (the name of which is long and very difficult to pronounce), and it came with many complications, including a heart problem. Our sweet girl had to be in the Neonatal Intensive Care Unit (NICU), but we were able to see her often and hold her. She was beautiful, small, strong, and greatly loved.

After just two weeks in the NICU, Dani was able to come home. We were so grateful, even though the future was still unknown. Doctors told us she wouldn't live very long, and a hospice nurse came to our house twice a week. Dani needed an oxygen tank to help her breathe easier whenever she slept. She wasn't able to nurse due to some latching difficulties, but I pumped milk and gave it to her in a bottle.

We continued to pray for Dani's healing. One of my favorite memories is when Mike would carry our baby girl in one hand as he prayed and read out loud from his Bible that was in the other hand. During that time of hospice and doctor visits, our family went about life as best we could. Dani slept in a bassinet near our bed in our room. We all went to church services, the mall, and restaurants. Mike and I even had a date one afternoon when a NICU nurse offered to watch Dani.

Two months after she was born, our little warrior seemed to be tiring of fighting. She struggled to drink from her little bottle, and her breathing grew increasingly labored. Her tiny body would stiffen as if to stretch, which the doctor later determined to be seizures. Dani's time with us appeared to be coming to an end.

We took her to the hospital, hoping that something could be done to extend her life. The doctor and nurses did everything they could. Mike and I took turns lying next to her on the hospital bed throughout the night. By morning, Dani was burning with fever. We held her, told her how much we loved her, and promised that she would always be with us in our hearts. Around 4:30 in the afternoon, surrounded by people who loved her, Dani went to heaven.

Mike's mom, my dad, and several close family friends were present as Mike, Jacob, Joel, and I said goodbye. Shortly after, the hospital room filled with many more loved ones who had prayed with us through this season. We left the hospital that evening knowing Dani was with the Lord. Our hearts ached as we began to think about planning a funeral. This was not the ending we had prayed for, but we knew we had been blessed to have Dani in our lives. Our precious girl defied so many odds during her short time on earth, and she forever changed us.

Every year on her birthday in July, our family celebrates Dani's life, and in September, we commemorate the day she went to heaven. Our daughter lived for only two months and six days, but she touched many lives. Her story has brought hope and joy to families who have gone through similar situations. Mike and I have also been able to help couples navigate the grief and despair of losing a child. While this is not the kind of ministry one hopes to experience personally, we have been honored and blessed to help others in their times of loss.

During Dani's time with us and even after she passed away, it was important to me that the atmosphere of our home did not change. I didn't want Jacob and Joel to see this season

27

as one of sorrow and anxiety. I wanted them to know that because of our faith in Jesus Christ, we could still have joy and peace, even in the midst of pain and tears. (And there were many, many tears after Dani went to heaven.) I had to make the decision not to live in sadness and pain. I didn't want my sons to look back at this time and think, *Mom used to be so silly and happy, but she changed after our sister died.* The promises of God were still true, and they gave me the strength to move forward and be grateful for the opportunity to know and love our girl.

WORDS FROM THE LORD

Several months after Dani passed away, I was preparing to speak at a mother's luncheon. I remembered what my friend had said about getting a word for my baby, and I asked God for a word for each of my children.

For our first baby, whom we lost early in the pregnancy, the word I received was "I (God) am in control." I learned that I have no control over what happens in my life. Yes, I make many decisions on a daily basis, but ultimately, God is in control of everything. I can choose to trust Him, or I can try to manipulate my circumstances. The first choice brings peace; the second brings stress. I choose to trust God.

> I can choose to trust Him, or I can try to manipulate my circumstances. The first choice brings peace; the second brings stress.

For Jacob, the Lord gave me the word "joy." This word describes our firstborn son perfectly. He seldom lets anything get him down. He always finds a way to see the bright side of every situation and the good in every person. Jacob is so full of joy, and he is a blessing and an encouragement to everyone in his life.

For Joel, the Lord gave me the word "love." God knew he would be one who loves deeply and whose smile makes everyone around him feel loved and welcome. Joel has a soft heart towards those who are downtrodden and forgotten. He is sensitive to the feelings of others. I'm thankful for his tender heart and reminded to really "see" those around me.

For Jared, the Lord gave me the word "strength." God's power and strength carried me through the loss of our son, and the strength of those around our family helped us feel cared for and loved. Jared also gave me a greater appreciation for my children. I was more thankful than ever for Jacob and Joel, and I had a renewed energy and excitement about being their mom.

For Dani, the Lord gave me the word "miracle." Merriam-Webster's Dictionary defines miracle as "an extraordinary event manifesting divine intervention in human affairs."[1] I would define Dani's life in such a way. Medically speaking, she was not supposed to live, but she did! I know with all my heart that God made a way for her to come into this world, and her short life impacted many families and continues to do so.

When God gave me the word "miracle" for Dani, I thought it meant she would be healed. But she was still our miracle gift, even though she was only with us for a short time. Perhaps one of the miracles was that we (Mike, the boys, and I) survived. Our faith was strengthened, and our hearts, though sad, continued to trust God and His Word.

---

1. *Merriam-Webster.com Dictionary*, s.v. "miracle," accessed June 24, 2020, https://www.merriam-webster.com/dictionary/miracle.

One day I asked Jacob and Joel what words came to mind when they thought of their sister. They said love, peace, and joy. This response amazed me. During the time Dani was home with us, we had numerous doctor appointments and hospice visits. Whenever we left the house, we had to bring an oxygen tank with us. It was not what you would consider a "normal" life, yet our sons saw love, peace and joy. I believe it's because we submitted our life to God in prayer. We chose to walk in joy, despite our sadness. We chose to walk in love instead of fear, and we made the decision to live victoriously instead of defeated.

MY DAUGHTERS-IN-LOVE

Jacob and Joel are now grown and married, and I have two daughters-in-love. These women are beautiful, inside and out, and I am so thankful for them. They are the precious blessings I prayed for from the time my sons were born.

In 2015, Jacob married Neeli. She is creative, musical, and artistic, and she has a lifestyle videography business. She is madly in love with God and Jacob. Neeli is strong in character and genuine in all she says and does. Family and friends are important to her heart. Confident in who she is in Christ, Neeli encourages me to remember who I am in the Lord.

Our son Joel married his bride in 2019. She is artistic, loves all things music, and has a stationery and calligraphy business. Her name is Danielle, but she goes by Danny. I tell her that she is not a replacement for Baby Dani, she is a bonus! Danny has a huge heart for others. She cares deeply for family and honors everyone in her life. Her affectionate nature is the perfect complement to Joel's tender heart. Their favorite place is wherever they are together.

Having daughters-in-love is one of my greatest joys. The word I have for Neeli and Danny is "treasure". These lovely ladies are of great worth and value to me and our family. Seeing our sons and their wives setting up their own homes, loving each other, and loving God is this mom's dream come true!

CHAPTER 2

STUDY GUIDE

REVIEW

When I became a Christian, the Lord opened my heart to becoming a mom. There have been many wonderful moments filled with joy, and there have also been some difficult times of sadness and confusion. I am blessed to have two wonderful sons (and two lovely daughters-in-love) on earth as well as three precious babies in heaven. In every season, God has been faithful to our family.

SCRIPTURES

- Psalm 28:6–8
- Psalm 127:3–4
- Psalm 139:13–16
- Proverbs 3:5–6

QUESTIONS

- Before you had children, what were your thoughts or concerns about becoming a mom?
- What are some examples of God's faithfulness to your family?
- As a mom and a follower of Jesus Christ, in what areas would you like to grow and mature?

HEART CONNECTORS

- Ask the Lord for a word for each of your children. (If you have children in heaven, you can still ask for a word for them. It's a wonderful way to remember and honor their lives.) God will speak to your heart and mind. He may give you a single word, a phrase, or even a picture. Record it in your journal and write what it says about your child. Thank the Lord for allowing you to be your children's mom.

- Set aside some one-on-one time with each of your children and share the word you received from the Lord. Remind them that you love them and that you are so proud and thankful to be their mom. Let them know you pray for them every day.

PRAYER

Father God, thank You that I am Your child. Your love never ceases to amaze me. Thank You, Lord, for my precious children. I know that each one is a special gift from You. Please give me wisdom, strength, and peace for each new day. I need Your help to be the best mother I can be. In Jesus' name, Amen.

CHAPTER 3

THE PERFECT MOM

God arms me with strength,
and he makes my way perfect.

—Psalm 18:32

W hen we brought Jacob home from the hospital, my goal was to be a great mom and wife. I wanted my son to be happy and fed and my house to be clean and organized. Surely it couldn't be that difficult, right? However, I failed to account for one significant factor—sleep deprivation.

One day I walked into our bedroom, and the radio was on. (Yes, we still listened to the radio in the 90s.) Someone was talking about motherhood, and they said the most important person in a young son's life is his mother. Some women might find this idea encouraging, but to me, it was an impossibly high demand. I sat on the edge of the bed and started crying. It wasn't just a few tears either. No, I ugly cried. (Sobs, gasps for air, so many tissues—the works).

Mike came in and found me falling apart. All I could think was, *God, what were You thinking? How will I ever be able to be a good mom? My poor son. How am I going to do this?* After a little while, I finally calmed down enough to share these fears with my husband. Mike lovingly reminded me that I was going to be alright and so was Jacob. With God's help, we would all be just fine.

THE PERFECT MOM

If you asked 100 people to define the "perfect" mom, I can almost guarantee you would receive 100 different definitions. Why? Because everyone looks at motherhood differently. One person may say a perfect mom is someone who is always happy and smiling. Someone else may say it's the mom who keeps her house spotless, and yet another may say it's the mom who has the best-behaved children.

Personally, I don't think there is a single definition of the perfect mom. Every woman is uniquely designed by God with a special combination of strengths, gifts, and abilities. Why does this matter? Because He knows exactly what kind of mother your children need. No two children are exactly the same. Each one has areas in which they will excel and areas in which they will need extra help. God equips every mother with the specific tools she needs to help her children grow into loving, mature adults.

When I began my journey into motherhood, I prayed that everything I said and did would bring my children closer to the Lord. I was not a perfect mom at the beginning, and I'm still not perfect today. So why did I decide to write a book on being a mom and offer parenting advice? That's easy—I love being a mom. Every season has been a blessing. The Lord gave me such a desire and joy for motherhood that I want to bless and encourage other moms on their journey.

Mike and I love our children, and we have always sought to follow what God's Word says about parenting. Does this mean we did everything the right way the first time? Were our sons perfect angels who always obeyed and never experienced any challenges? The answer to both questions is no. There have been times when we definitely missed the parenting mark, and our sons have had their own share of missteps.

Here is the good news: our lack of perfection does not alter who God is or what His Word says.

> **Our lack of perfection does not alter who God is or what His Word says.**

The faithful love of the LORD never ends!
    His mercies never cease.
Great is his faithfulness;
    his mercies begin afresh each morning
    (Lamentations 3:22–23).

God loves us, and He will never stop loving us. Every day brings new mercy for our children and for us as parents. No human parent will get everything right all the time, and that is okay. God is already the perfect Father, and His plans for us are perfect too.

I am so grateful for God's kindness to our family. He covered all my shortcomings and gave me wisdom for every season. My greatest joy as a mother is that my sons know and love God. They believe He has wonderful plans for their lives and have no doubt that they are deeply and unconditionally loved.

SAY GOODBYE TO DISCOURAGEMENT

Parenting. This word can bring both joy and fear to moms and dads alike. Why? I believe it's because the enemy wants us to be fearful *for* our children and *of* our children. He wants us to be afraid that we won't know what to do, that we're going to mess up, and that our days are going to be really difficult.

One thing I noticed early on as a mom was the discouragement that so many parents feel. Mike and I talked about this, and we asked ourselves two questions:

1. Why do so many parents find themselves discouraged?
2. Why do so many *Christian* parents find themselves discouraged?

In my opinion, the answer is the same for both questions. Many parents don't read the Bible, or if they do, it's only when circumstances have become really bad. Consequently, they don't know that God offers comfort and wisdom for every day in His Word.

> Joyful are people of integrity,
>> who follow the instructions of the LORD.
> Joyful are those who obey his laws
>> and search for him with all their hearts (Psalm 119:1–2).

Discouragement is defeated when we surrender control to the Lord and allow Him to fill us with encouragement through His Word and His presence. God is all-knowing and all-powerful, and He is available to help us every moment of every day. We just have to ask!

Is it okay to seek guidance from friends and family too? Yes, it certainly is. God designed us to live in relationship with one another, and having godly people you can ask for help is a huge blessing. You can also find advice from wonderful Christian moms in magazines and books and on social media and blogs. However, be cautious that you do not allow human opinions to have more authority in your life than God's Word. The Bible is the ultimate authority on what is true and right. In a world where information is simply a click or phone call away, we need

> **Be cautious that you do not allow human opinions to have more authority in your life than God's Word.**

to be watchful that the counsel we allow to shape our lives lines up with what God has to say.

It is true that as parents, we won't always know what to do, and we will make mistakes. Our little ones (and not so little ones) are hard work! Training children to be loving, respectful, and obedient takes time, energy, and a whole lot of prayer.

Here is something else that is equally true: your children will bring you tremendous joy. They will help you learn to hear God's voice as you seek His counsel and direction for your family. They will help your faith grow stronger as you spend time in prayer, asking for wisdom and strength. Most importantly, your children help you remember how much God loves you. When your heart swells with love at the sight of their faces, it will be a reminder of how much the Lord loves them and you. How amazing is that?

NO NEED TO HURRY

One of the saddest things I've seen over the years is that far too many parents believe they're supposed to suffer through parenting. The enemy would have us believe our children are a bother and a barrier to enjoying life. Consequently, there are moms and dads who can't wait until their children are old enough to move out of the house.

I do believe it is important to encourage children to grow, mature, and seek God's plan for their future. As parents, we can absolutely enjoy the process of helping them grow in their strengths and abilities. However, it is also important to recognize and celebrate each season with your young ones. Please don't mentally rush them out the door. Every stage of growth brings new opportunities for encouragement, training, and connection. Perhaps the one thing your heart needs to hear today is *you can enjoy life right now with your children.* Yes, there will be challenging moments. Some ages and stages of development may bring you to your knees in prayer (and exhaustion). With God's help, though, you can treasure your family through all of it. Your children will eventually leave home one day, and you will be grateful for the precious time you had to lay a strong foundation of love and faith in their lives.

CALLED TO PERFECT LOVE

In Matthew 5, Jesus begins His famous "Sermon on the Mount," in which He teaches on many important aspects of being His follower. He says in verse 44, "Love your enemies! Pray for those who persecute you." Sounds like a tall order, doesn't it? You may have people in your life you would classify as "enemies," and if you don't, there are still probably some individuals you prefer to avoid. How can you love them?

The answer is in verse 48: "You are to be perfect, even as your Father in heaven is perfect." In this context, "perfect" does not mean flawless or without sin, because that would be an impossible task for any human. We all make mistakes. "Perfect" in this verse means "finished, complete, pure, holy."[2] When we are born again, God makes us complete through His Son, Jesus. He gives us the power to love people like He does—wholly, unconditionally, and unendingly.

You don't have to be a "perfect" mom to have this perfect love. Your words and actions will have a much greater impact on your children than a decorated house, fancy clothes, or expensive toys. Ask the Lord to show you His heart for the people in your life and choose to love them as God loves you.

---

2. Albert Barnes, "Matthew 5: Barnes' Notes," Bible Hub, accessed July 2, 2020, https://biblehub.com/commentaries/barnes/matthew/5.htm.

///////

I recently spoke with a woman who was experiencing a difficult situation with her child. She was frustrated and overwhelmed, and she questioned every parenting decision she had ever made. As a mom I understood her pain and confusion—I've experienced the same doubts and felt the same sting of inadequacy.

The Lord gave me a wonderful picture of encouragement to share with this woman. I said, "None of us get 'being Mom' perfectly." I asked her to imagine making a list of all the things she believed she had done wrong. Then I said, "Imagine the hand of God dipping a huge paint brush at the foot of the cross where the blood of Jesus was flowing down. See the Lord taking that blood-soaked brush and swiping it up and down over that list of mistakes." I went on to encourage her that all our past, current, and future mistakes are covered by the blood of Jesus.

> **All our past, current, and future mistakes are covered by the blood of Jesus.**

I believe every mom (including me!) needs to hear that encouragement and anchor it in her heart. Motherhood can be really hard sometimes, and so can life in general. Sickness. Rebellion. Drugs. Pornography. Anger. Divorce. Death. The list goes on and on. Whatever your situation may be, God is there for you. His love for you cannot and will not end. The blood of Jesus covers all your mistakes, and you are free from shame. I pray these words of the apostle Paul will bring hope and healing to your heart:

I am convinced that nothing can ever separate us from God's love. Neither death nor life, neither angels nor demons, neither our fears for today nor our worries about tomorrow—not even the powers of hell can separate us from God's love. No power in the sky above or in the earth below—indeed, nothing in all creation will ever be able to separate us from the love of God that is revealed in Christ Jesus our Lord (Romans 8:38–39).

CHAPTER 3

STUDY GUIDE

REVIEW

God designs every mother with the perfect combination of strengths, gifts, and abilities to help her children. He is also faithful to cover our mistakes and give us encouragement through His Word. Some moments will be more challenging than others, but we can choose to treasure every stage with our children. As we grow in our relationship with God, we will begin to reflect His perfect love for our family and for the world around us.

SCRIPTURES

- Psalm 119
- Psalm 143:8–10
- Luke 6:34–36
- Hebrews 13:19–21

QUESTIONS

- What were your expectations when you first became a mom? Did you have to make any adjustments?
- How would you encourage a friend who feels pressure to be a "perfect" mom?
- What are some exciting milestones you can look forward to as your children experience new stages of development?

HEART CONNECTORS

- Write a letter to each of your children, telling them three specific things you love about them and why they are so special to you. Record this message in your journal so you will have a copy, and then send the letter in the mail.

- In your quiet time, ask the Lord to show you if there is anything keeping you from loving others like He does. He may bring a person to your mind whom you need to forgive or a situation that you need to address. It might be uncomfortable at first, but don't shy away from His voice. Remember, God loves you and wants the best for you. He wants to set you free to love people the way He does.

PRAYER

Father God, thank You for Your wonderful kindness to my family. I am not a perfect mom, despite my best intentions, and I need Your help every day. Thank You for the blood of Jesus that covers all my mistakes. When discouragement tries to fill my heart, please remind me that I can find comfort and joy in Your presence. I pray that my children will see Your perfect love through my words and actions and that they will fall deeply in love with You. In Jesus' name, Amen.

HEART HOLDERS

Guard your heart above all else,
for it determines the course of your life.

—Proverbs 4:23

W hen my sons were young, I often asked them, "Do I have your heart?" Mike and I knew the world was full of things vying for our children's attention and affections, and we didn't want their hearts being pulled away from us or from God's best for their lives. Our hope was to hold their hearts until they gave them to the Lord. This heart transplant is the most important thing that will ever happen in a person's life.

HOW DO I HOLD THEIR HEARTS?

Do everything with love (1 Corinthians 16:14).

Being kind and loving will always go a long way in any relationship, and this is certainly true with our children. Now, you may be thinking, *Of course I'm loving and kind to my children. I'm their mother!* I have no doubt you love your children, but I also know from experience that it can be difficult to maintain a loving and kind disposition all day long when you have a house to clean, errands to run, and school functions and sports activities to attend. Whether you homeschool your children or work outside the home, you are probably a very busy lady!

So how can you still be loving and kind in the middle of all that busyness? I believe the key to holding your children's hearts is to be sure that your own heart is in tune with the Lord. When we are in sync with Him, our words, actions, and attitudes will line up as well.

> **The key to holding your children's hearts is to be sure that your own heart is in tune with the Lord.**

Many moms have asked me, "How do I get my children's hearts?" I think what they really want to know is *How can I have a heart connection with my children so that they will listen to me and do what I ask*? It certainly is nice when our children promptly do what they are told. However, if they're only obeying to avoid consequences, then the obedience will be short-lived and will do nothing for our parent-child relationship. That is why having your children's hearts is so important. When you have their hearts, they obey because they know obedience is the right thing to do.

HEART-TO-HEART CONNECTION

As moms, we want to create an atmosphere of love and togetherness that will lead to heart-to-heart connections with our families. Let's explore some ways we can connect with the hearts of our children. (By the way, even if your children are grown, it's never too late to work on your connection. You may need to be a bit creative, but the Lord will give you wisdom and help you build healthy relationships with your adult children.)

SET A GODLY EXAMPLE

And you yourself must be an example to them by doing good works of every kind. Let everything you do reflect the integrity and seriousness of your teaching (Titus 2:7).

Admit Your Mistakes

Many years ago, Mike and I were preparing to do our very first teaching on parenting. Our sons were about nine and seven years old at the time. A few days before the class, I sat down to finalize our notes, and one of the boys started asking me questions. At first, I was like, "Uh-huh ... okay ... I'll be there in a minute." He kept on talking, though, until I finally looked up and not-so-lovingly responded, "I AM WORKING ON A TEACHING ON PARENTING! GIVE ME SOME TIME!"

As soon as the words left my mouth, I felt embarrassed and convicted. How could I teach other people to be gracious, loving parents when I still had so much to learn? I wish I could tell you that moment was a one-time mistake and from then on I always responded to my sons with patience and understanding. However, as I mentioned in the previous chapter, I am not a perfect mom—I made plenty of mistakes (and still do today). I did learn a crucial lesson, though. I learned how to say "I'm sorry. I was wrong."

Everything we do as parents tells our children something about their heavenly Father. When we admit our flaws and ask for their forgiveness, we teach them that everyone makes mistakes and needs God's grace. When we forgive our children for their mistakes, we demonstrate how God is faithful to forgive us when we repent and turn away from our sins.

One of the most important things we can teach our children is that mistakes do not lessen God's love for us or our love for each other. Love is not something we have to earn, nor is it

> Everything we do as parents tells our children something about their heavenly Father.

something we have to worry about losing. God loves us because He made us, and we love our children because they are part of us. Nothing will ever change that. When our children know and believe this, they will feel safe to share their hearts with both God and us.

Ask for Help

I once read something that both convicted and challenged me as a mother and a Christian. It was a simple question: *would I be satisfied if my children grew up to have the same kind of walk with the Lord that I have?* I had to pause and honestly examine my heart. Could I answer with a definite "yes"? Or were there any areas in my spiritual life that were lacking?

That kind of introspection can be scary! And it's not a one-time thing either. I think most (if not all) Christians go through ups and downs in their relationship with God, feeling close and confident during some seasons but distant and discouraged in others. During the hard times, we may even wonder, *How can God love me when I am such a mess?*

Please allow me to encourage you with this truth: mess or no mess, God loves you. He wants you to live in the freedom Christ died on the cross to give you. If there is an area of weakness in your life, don't try to hide it or ignore it. Go to your heavenly Father and ask Him to help you. Then confide in some trustworthy, godly friends. I am thankful for the women in my life who have patiently heard my cries and even cried with me. They have prayed for me and encouraged me through many situations. I have also had the blessing of receiving wise counsel from leaders at my church.

Asking for help doesn't make you a bad Christian or a bad mom. We all need help sometimes. By admitting your struggles, you show that you care not only about your own spiritual health but also about the spiritual health of your family. Your commitment to growing in your relationship with the Lord will bless your children and encourage them to grow too.

Make the Lord Part of Your Everyday Life

The Bible

Teaching your children about the importance of the Bible does not have to wait until they can read. When they are babies, you can read Bible stories to them. When they are a little older, you can give them their own children's Bibles. My sons were around three and five years old when I began family quiet times. Every afternoon at 2 pm, Jacob and Joel would go to their rooms. They did not know how to read yet, but they could color in their Bible story coloring books or look at the pictures in their children's Bibles. Sometimes they took naps, but this was a way of training them to have daily quiet times of their own. Although our 2 pm quiet times eventually changed as the boys grew older, they did help my sons understand the significance of setting aside time to be with the Lord and read His Word.

Throughout the time my sons lived at home, I intentionally read my Bible in places where they could see me (the living room, the dining room, etc.). I wanted them to know that when I talked about the importance of reading God's Word, I meant it. I also regularly shared verses I had read and how God used them to speak to me. Once the boys were a little older, I sometimes invited them to join me in my Bible reading time. I read to them, and they read to me. These were special moments in which our hearts connected with God and each other.

Prayer

Ever since Mike and I got saved, prayer has been very important to us. We taught our sons to pray about all kinds of things. We always prayed before meals, and whenever we heard a siren, we prayed for everyone involved. We prayed for family, friends, and anyone else we knew who was sick or in a tough situation. Prayer was not just something we did at night when the boys went to bed. No, it was (and continues to be) a regular, normal, and indispensable part of our lives.

Make it a priority to include your children in your prayer times whenever possible. They can pray for meals, for family and friends, and for anything else that is on their minds. Siblings can pray for each other as well. When brothers and sisters pray for each other out loud, it helps build their relationship. Teach your children that they can talk to God anytime, just like you can. He loves them and wants to talk to them too!

Praise and Worship

An easy way to share Jesus with your little ones is to play praise and worship music at home and in the car. There are many great Christian songs available for every age. You can also include songs as part of your children's bedtime routine.

When I was pregnant with Jacob, I imagined how wonderful it was going to be to sing songs to him as I rocked him to sleep. I pictured myself in the light blue nursery, sitting in the rocking chair Mike had painted for me. It was a beautiful dream. In reality, though, Jacob never seemed to enjoy being sung to when he was rocked. I soon gave that up. When Joel joined our family, I think I tried it again. (I have to admit that those early days of having a newborn and a toddler are a bit of a blur.)

When the boys were about four and two years old, I tried bedtime songs once again, this time with much more success.

There were a couple of songs that became part of our regular nighttime routine. I inserted the boys' names when singing "Jesus Loves the Little Children," and I added my own words here and there. It was a sweet, fun way to end the day, and I think I enjoyed this time even more than my sons did. (But I promise they really did like it!)

Grateful Attitudes

Have you ever heard the phrase, "More is caught than taught."? I believe this is true when it comes to having a grateful attitude. As parents, our gratefulness in everyday situations provides a godly example for our children to follow.

God's Word tells us, "Be thankful in all circumstances" (1Thessalonians 5:18). Note that it doesn't say to be thankful "for" the circumstances but "in" them. Life on this earth has many challenges and difficulties, but you have a wonderful heavenly Father who cares for you and watches over you. When you thank Him for His strength, wisdom, and peace, you develop a grateful attitude that impacts the atmosphere of your home and influences the hearts of your children.

Does this mean you don't need to talk to your children about gratitude? Not at all. It is important to teach them, especially when they are young, why they should be grateful and how to show it. Mike and I taught our young sons to be grateful for every gift they received and to always say "Thank you." Before their birthdays or other gift-giving holidays, we helped them practice how to respond when opening presents. If they received something they already had, the correct response was "Thank you." If they received something they didn't like, the correct response was "Thank you." And if they received something our family wouldn't watch or listen to in our home, the correct response was still "Thank you."

Mike and I weren't trying to control or manipulate our sons. They didn't have to like or even use every gift they received.

Some presents simply did not fit within our family's values. However, our sons could always be grateful that other people spent money, time, and energy to send them gifts. That is why we taught them to say "Thank you" no matter what.

Tithes, Offerings, and Giving

In *The Blessed Life*, Pastor Robert Morris writes about God's heart for tithes and offerings. Perhaps you have never thought about how your relationship with God intersects with your finances, and if that is the case, I highly encourage you to read that book. Tithing is giving the first 10 percent of your gross earnings to God through your home church. It is an act of obedience found throughout the Bible (read Deuteronomy 14:22 and Malachi 3:10 for starters), and it comes with a promise of blessing for all who obey.

Anything given to God beyond the first 10 percent is an offering. Some churches have special projects for which they take up an offering, but you can give to God anytime. It is a way to demonstrate your thankfulness to Him for His provision.

Pastor Robert also encourages readers to listen to God's voice about giving to others. God may direct you to bless someone financially or in any number of other ways (time, energy, talents, etc.). Be aware that in these moments, the enemy will try to put doubts in your mind, such as "You barely have enough for your own family" or "That gift is way too extravagant." When those thoughts come, remind yourself that God is faithful and has good plans for you. As you obediently bless others, you can trust that He will take care of you every step of the way. Pastor Robert concludes *The Blessed Life* with these encouraging words:

> Giving when the Lord leads, helping people know the love and goodness of God, keeping the focus on God rather than on things, being generous, and allowing God to do a work in

our hearts are the keys to making our journey on earth an adventure of joy and purpose.[3]

How can you apply all of this to parenting? Teach your children what the Bible says about tithes and offerings. Tell them you are happy to obey God because everything you have comes from Him. When the situation permits, allow your children to see you giving to other people. Explain to them that when you have a thankful heart, giving to others is a blessing to you too!

When our sons were old enough to understand the value of money, Mike and I gave them a weekly allowance. Now, some families connect allowances with chores, but in our house, we kept the two separate. Our boys were expected to help around the house because that was simply part of doing life with our family. (We did, however, bless the boys with a bonus if they did a big job.) Our reason for giving them an allowance was to help them learn the principles of tithes and offerings as well as the importance of giving to others and saving for the future.

TEACH AND SHARE BIBLICAL TRUTH

When should we teach our children about the Lord? We find the answer in Deuteronomy 11:9:

> Teach them [God's commands] to your children. Talk about them when you are at home and when you are on the road, when you are going to bed and when you are getting up.

This verse gives us four times and places to instruct our children:

---

3. Robert Morris, *The Blessed Life* (Southlake, TX; Gateway Publishing, 2019), 177.

1. When we are at home
2. When we are on the road (out and about)
3. When we get ready for bed
4. When we wake up

You may think, *That is practically the entire day!* And you are right. God wants us to talk about Him with our children all the time. I believe He directs us to do this so our children will know that He has always been faithful in the past and that they can trust Him for the present and the future.

Here are some practical ways you can teach and share biblical truth with your children:

Pray Often and Everywhere

Yes, I know I already mentioned prayer in this chapter, but I cannot emphasize enough how important it really is. One of my favorite ways to pray is to declare Scriptures over my family and the various situations in our lives. By doing this, I am agreeing with God's Word, and that is powerful!

Family prayer times are a great way to teach your children how to talk to God. Tell your children about family members or friends who are sick or going through difficult circumstances. (Details should, of course, be age-appropriate.) Then invite your children to pray out loud for these needs. These prayers don't have to be long or complicated—they can be as simple as "God, please help Grandma feel better." Tell your children that God loves it when they talk to Him and that He always hears their prayers.

Allowing your children to participate in family prayer times helps them become confident in their prayer lives, and it also gives them opportunities to see God move in the lives of others. When a prayer for a sick loved one is answered, you can rejoice as a family in their healing. If a prayer is not answered as hoped for, then your family can come alongside that loved one with comfort and support. Your children will learn that God is good even during the most difficult times. They will come to understand that God is loving, kind, and faithful—not because of what He does, but because of who He is.

Allowing your children to participate in family prayer times helps them become confident in their prayer lives, and it also gives them opportunities to see God move in the lives of others.

Both of our sons lived at home until they got married, and Mike and I made it a priority to pray with them before they went to bed. If we were out of town, we would call and pray with them over the phone. With the exception of the seasons they were dating their now-wives, we hardly ever missed a night when we all prayed together. These nightly prayer times addressed any particular areas of need (such as health and wisdom) and always included our personal version of the priestly blessing in Numbers 6:24–26.

The LORD bless you
    and keep you;
the LORD make his face shine on you
    and be gracious to you;
the LORD turn his face toward you
    and give you peace (NIV).

We spoke this blessing over our sons from the time they were very young until the nights before they each got married.

Make God "Real"

Sometimes it is difficult for young children to understand what is real and what is pretend. For example, if you read a fun fiction story and a Bible story to your little ones, they may believe both stories are equally true. How can you help them know the difference? Begin by telling them what you are reading. If you're reading a fiction book, then tell your children, "This story did not actually happen, but it's fun to use your imagination." There may even be a lesson or teaching point you can share. For a non-fiction book, let them know that the story really did happen. Autobiographies and biographies are great ways to introduce your children to Christian men and women who chose to stand for truth and live for God, despite their struggles and mistakes.

When you read the Bible, tell your children that everything in God's Word is true. It's a book that is filled with amazing stories and adventures, and every time we read it, we can learn something new! Make reading the Bible an enjoyable experience for your children. Before you know it, they will be reading and enjoying Bible stories on their own. Most importantly, they discovered that God is real and that He always loves us and takes care of us.

Find Teachable Moments

My sons used to roll their eyes during my "That reminds me of sin" phase. I would jokingly (and sometimes not jokingly) take any word, phrase, or situation and talk about how it could relate to sin. It was primarily meant to be fun, but it also helped me teach the boys biblical truths.

Children are full of questions about life. Whenever possible, point them back to the Scriptures. The goal is not to sound "preachy" but to let your children know that the Bible can help us understand the world around us. By the way, telling your children to read the Bible is good, but reading it with them as you sit side by side is better. Sitting with them makes you available to answer any questions they might have. And if you don't know an answer, you can look it up together.

> **Telling your children to read the Bible is good, but reading it with them as you sit side by side is better.**

There will probably be times when your children have trouble understanding what they are reading, and they may even express some doubts. That's okay! By allowing them to talk freely about their struggles, you will create an environment of trust and safety, and you will also learn what to pray for them. Encourage your children to keep reading God's Word and to ask their heavenly Father to help them understand His heart.

Build Altars

Throughout the Old Testament, the people of Israel built altars as memorials of the times God met with them and did miraculous things in their lives. Consequently, they not only reminded people of what God had done in their lifetime, but they also taught future generations about His faithfulness.

The first thing the Israelites did upon entering the Promised Land was build such a reminder:

> Joshua called together the twelve men he had chosen—one from each of the tribes of Israel. He told them, "Go into the middle of the Jordan, in front of the Ark of the LORD your God. Each of you must pick up one stone and carry it out

on your shoulder—twelve stones in all, one for each of the twelve tribes of Israel. We will use these stones to build a memorial. In the future your children will ask you, 'What do these stones mean?' Then you can tell them, 'They remind us that the Jordan River stopped flowing when the Ark of the LORD's Covenant went across.' These stones will stand as a memorial among the people of Israel forever" (Joshua 4:4–7).

What are your family's reminders of God's presence and faithfulness during difficult times? Altars made of stone may not be practical or possible for you, but here are some modern-day options:

- Journals
- Photographs and videos
- Cards and letters
- Scrapbooks and memory books

These mementos can serve as starting points for conversations with your children (and future generations) about God and how He has been a part of your lives.

In our master bedroom closet, I have a box that contains the clothes I wore at the hospital on the day our baby daughter, Dani, passed away. It also holds the outfit she was wearing. At first, I really didn't know why I kept these things. I would open the box on the anniversary of the day Dani went to heaven, and I would cry as I remembered her small and beautiful hands and feet. Over the years, the Lord has brought great comfort and peace to my heart, and the box no longer represents her death. Instead, it is a sweet altar that reminds me of our baby girl's short but precious life and the love she brought to our family. I still cry a little on her anniversary day, but I smile more.

My mom passed away almost 20 years ago. When I went to help my dad with the funeral arrangements, he asked me to go through her personal things to see if there was anything I wanted to keep. I had never known my mom to be overly sentimental, but as I searched through her closets and drawers, I found a box of pictures and papers. As an only child, there were quite a few pictures of me, but what struck me the most was that my mom had also kept the cards and letters I sent to her when I was grown and married. As a young woman, I competed in pageants, and she had kept all the pictures and pamphlets from the events, as well as a couple of crowns. I was surprised and so touched that she had done this. She had kept an altar—not one of adoration but one of remembrance of a season in my life.

As a mother myself, I have kept many of the drawings my sons made during their childhood. Even more endearing is the "gold and silver" jewelry they gave me during their younger years. These pieces are not as gold and silver as they used to be, but they are priceless in my eyes. Now that my sons are grown, I cherish every note, card, and picture I have of them and their wonderful wives. These mementos serve as sweet remembrances of their adult lives and memorials of God's continued faithfulness to our family.

SHARE TESTIMONIES

Similar to altars, testimonies are stories about what God has done in your life. Sharing testimonies with your children is not only fun, but it also helps them understand what makes your family so special.

> We will not hide these truths from our children;
>   we will tell the next generation
> about the glorious deeds of the LORD,
>   about his power and his mighty wonders.

For he issued his laws to Jacob;
    he gave his instructions to Israel.
He commanded our ancestors
    to teach them to their children,
so the next generation might know them—
    even the children not yet born—
and they in turn will teach their own children.
    So each generation should set its hope anew on God,
not forgetting his glorious miracles
    and obeying his commands (Psalm 78:4–7).

One of our favorite family testimonies is about our son Joel. When he was around four years old, he would complain sometimes about discomfort in his leg. At first, Mike and I thought it was just growing pains. One evening at dinner, though, some friends of ours shared that they knew a couple whose son had leg pain, and it turned out to be part of a serious illness. Mike and I decided it was time to take Joel to our family doctor. X-rays revealed a spot on his hip, and an MRI was needed to determine what that spot was.

Now Mike was still playing professional golf at that time, and he had to be out of town the day of the MRI. My friend Debbie took us to the hospital that morning. Upon arriving, Joel and I were taken into a patient room where he was prepped "for the exam." My son was pretty tough for a four-year-old, and he did not act very nervous at all. I, on the other hand, had been crying out to the Lord and praying fervently on my knees for Joel's healing during the weeks leading up to the test. Did I believe God could and would heal my son? Yes, I really did. But it was still hard to watch my little boy go through this experience.

The nurse gave Joel some medicine to make him sleepy and comfortable during the MRI. Soon, he was fast asleep, and the medical staff took him for the procedure. Debbie and I sat in the waiting room for what seemed like *forever*. Finally, the

MRI was finished, and I was allowed to go back to the patient room to be with my son. The nurse gave me a grape popsicle for Joel to have once he woke up. (It served as an incentive to get him to open his eyes.) Soon he was awake, eating his popsicle, and ready to leave.

Back home, I continued to pray. Several days later I received a call from the doctor with the MRI results. The spot on Joel's hip was gone! The doctor said it was a miracle. He didn't want to tell us before, but he had believed the spot was cancer. I told him we had the same thought, and we believed God healed our Joel.

Mike and I love encouraging others with this story, but we also realize that the person most impacted is Joel. After all, it's his testimony! This miracle helped lay the foundation of faith and trust in his life, and in moments of doubt, he can look back and remember the power and faithfulness of God.

I think it's important to remind ourselves that not all testimonies are the same, and one is not "better" than the next. When Dani was born with her chromosomal disorder, we prayed just as fervently for her healing as we did for Joel's. The outcome was very different, though, and we soon had to say goodbye to our baby girl. Did this mean God's faithfulness to our family somehow decreased? Not at all. Yes, it was a difficult time in our lives, but God's strength, love, and peace surrounded our family. There was not a single moment when He wasn't with us. We know we will see our baby girl again someday in heaven, and until then, we will share our family's testimony of God's goodness and faithfulness in *every* situation.

CREATE QUALITY TIME

When it comes to spending time as a family, it's often said that "quality, not quantity, counts." Personally, I love how my husband puts it: "Quality time happens within the quantity of time you spend with your family." The time we spend with our children from the cradle to adulthood will allow for more quality when we give more quantity. More time with our family equals more opportunities to share our hopes, our dreams, and our hearts. When that happens, we have the quality time we all desire.

> **Quality time happens within the quantity of time you spend with your family.**

Here are three ways to foster quality time:

Share Family Stories

When our sons were little, one of our birthday traditions was to tell them the stories of the days they were born. They loved hearing all about how Daddy took Mommy to the hospital and how excited we were to finally hold them in our arms.

There is something special about family stories. They connect the past with the present and bring the gift of togetherness. Over the last couple of years, there have been countless times that I've shared something with my married sons, and their responses have always been the same—"I never knew that about you." Isn't it amazing? Even after 30 years of marriage and over 26 years of being Mom, there are still stories to share. And these stories serve to bring us all closer, regardless of our children's ages.

Make Drive Time Divine Time

When our sons became involved in activities outside the house, we spent a lot of time in the car, driving here and there. I quickly realized that this was a unique opportunity to have a captive audience.

Make drive time divine time for your family. Ask your children open-ended questions that will give you a look into their hearts. Sometimes it's easier for our children to share with us when they're looking out the window and not directly at us. Here are some questions to help you get started:

- Who are your closest friends? What do you like about them?
- What is your favorite thing about yourself?
- How is school going? Is there a class you really like or dislike?
- If you could change anything in your world right now, what would it be?
- When you think about the future, what makes you excited?
- What are some things I can pray about for you?

Listen to your children and thank them for sharing with you. Let them know that what they have to say matters and is important to you. This may not be the time to give advice or direction. However, if you feel the need to discuss something further or give feedback, ask the Lord to give you wisdom. Tell your children that you love them, you are thankful they trusted you with their hearts, and your desire is to help them.

Always Be Available

Babies are famous for their middle of the night wake-up calls, but did you know that older and young adult children may keep you up late too? Our younger son, Joel, regularly wanted to share his heart after 10 pm. Tired or not, I was always available with a welcoming heart and an open ear. There were a few times I had to say "good night" around 2 am (yes, our talks went that late sometimes), but it was important to me that Joel knew he had my attention no matter how late it was. Mike usually had to go to bed a little earlier since he's not quite the night owl I am and he gets up pretty early. The significance of these late-night talks was that our son knew we were always there to listen, to give counsel (if asked), and to pray with and for him.

DO I HAVE YOUR HEART?

To ensure our children's hearts are open to us when they are older, we need be intentional about connecting with their hearts when they are young. Let me put it another way—if we want to be allowed into their adult world, then we first need to be present in their childhood world. As I mentioned at the beginning of this chapter, I often asked my young sons, "Do I have your heart?" This question served as an opening for anything we needed to talk about. One day Jacob told me that I seemed to be spending a lot of time serving in a particular ministry at church. I sensed he might be right. I truly loved that ministry, but after praying and talking to Mike, I stepped down because I knew it was the best thing for my family. A few years later, the Lord provided the opportunity for me to serve in that ministry again, and this time was the right time.

There are moments when we as moms need to reassess our priorities. It is easy to become involved with so many worthwhile activities outside the home that we begin to lose some footing in our family relationships. You may never have thought about it this way, but every mom works full time. Whether we work inside or outside our homes (or both), our time is limited. We want to be sure we are keeping our lives and hearts connected with those who are most important to us. We need to ask the Lord, "How do You want me to spend my time?" and then follow His direction.

As your children get older, there may be times when you feel a shift in the relationship. They are going to be maturing and learning to make some decisions on their own. This is a normal and healthy part of growing up, but it is also important to keep the lines of communication open should there be a concern that needs to be addressed. For example, there was a time when Mike and I felt our older son was being pulled away due to sports. Jacob was an avid tennis player during his teen and young adult years, and both he and Joel played competitively around the state. We began to notice that Jacob was spending more time playing tennis, practicing, and being coached than he was spending time at home. Mike and I were concerned, so we asked God to give us wisdom on how to approach the subject with our son. Jacob was about 13 or 14 years old at the time, and we didn't want to demand that he change his tennis schedule. Instead, we wanted to discuss the subject, hear his thoughts, and welcome him into the decision-making process.

The next day Jacob asked if we could talk. He said he wanted to make some changes in his schedule because he felt he was spending too much time with coaching and playing tennis. He wanted to cut back. We told Jacob we agreed with his decision, and he initiated the changes. What could have been a stressful issue was actually peaceful and easy because we took our concerns to the Lord and allowed Him to speak to our son's heart.

Situations may arise with our children in which we sense or see that their hearts are pulling away from us. This doesn't always signal a break in relationship, though. It can simply mean that they are learning to work things out on their own. If we as parents have set the example of going to the Lord in prayer for our life decisions, then our children will likely do the same. Our job, then, is to continue to seek the Lord in all we do and include our children in our pursuit of hearing God's direction. When we do this, we build on the foundation of trusting God and trusting each other.

We need to recognize that as they grow and mature, our children will have their own thoughts and perspectives on things. They aren't always going to agree with us on everything, and that's okay. What is not okay is for us as parents to try to force them to think the same way we do. It is also not okay for our children to disrespect or dishonor our input. What can you do if you see a rift developing in your relationship? First, pray for your children and ask God for wisdom in what to say and how to say it. Ask Him for strength, peace, and the perfect time to talk. Timing is everything—too early or too late in the day is rarely a good time for a heart-to-heart conversation. Keep in mind that what you see as a rift may only be a growing season for your children. Expect the best and be prayed up for anything that comes up.

> Timing is everything—too early or too late in the day is rarely a good time for a heart-to-heart conversation.

Growing up can be difficult and confusing for everyone involved. In tense moments, remind yourself of what the Bible says about love: "Love never gives up, never loses faith, is always hopeful, and endures through every circumstance" (1 Corinthians 13:7). It's crucial that your children know they are loved no matter what. Remind them that there is nothing they can say or do that will ever make you stop loving them. Let them know you are always available to talk, to pray, and even to sit and be silent together.

As your children see the Lord's goodness and faithfulness in your life, they will grow in their desire for Him. The more they love Him, the more their hearts become connected to His. And that is the ultimate goal of parenthood—to see your children totally surrender their hearts to the Lord.

STUDY GUIDE

REVIEW

In a world full of distractions, it is important to develop a heart-to-heart connection with your children. Begin by setting a godly example and making the Lord the most important part of your everyday life. Find practical ways to teach and share biblical truths and set aside moments to remember and rejoice in God's faithfulness. In every situation, remind your children that they are completely and unconditionally loved by you and by their heavenly Father.

SCRIPTURES

- Proverbs 4:4–13
- Proverbs 22:6
- Romans 12:9–16
- Philippians 4:8–9

QUESTIONS

- How do you feel about admitting your mistakes and asking for help? Who are some godly, trustworthy people you could confide in?
- What are some ways you can encourage your children to have grateful attitudes?

- Why is it important to share stories of God's faithfulness to your family?

HEART CONNECTORS

- A great way to make reading the Bible part of your daily routine is to read the book of Proverbs. There are 31 chapters, and by reading one chapter a day, you can complete the book every month. Make this a special time for your children. If they are too young to read, read out loud to them every day and choose one verse to talk about. If your children are old enough to read, you can take turns reading or have them read the chapter on their own. Then discuss it together at the end of the day.

- Think about the times when God has shown up and done miraculous things in your life. Write these memories in your journal and gather any mementos of the occasion (such as pictures, videos, letters, etc.). During family time, tell your children about God's faithfulness and allow them to look at the mementos. Remind your children that God never changes and that He will always be faithful to them too.

PRAYER

Father God, thank You for the privilege of being my children's mom. Please give me wisdom and help me direct their hearts to You instead of the things of this world. Lord, You are so faithful and good to our family. Even when things turn out differently than expected, we choose to trust You. May we grow to know and love You more every day. In Jesus' name, Amen.

CHAPTER 5

INTENTIONAL INVESTMENTS

Start children off on the way they should go,
and even when they are old they will not turn from it.
—Proverbs 22:6 NIV

I'm encouraged every time I read the above verse. As parents, we're to start off our sons and daughters on their way. How exciting! But on their way to where? Thinking about all the possibilities for our children's future is fun and exciting, especially when we recognize their special giftings and talents. However, Scripture tells us we're to get them started on the way *they* should go. In other words, it's not our choice to make. We should never try to force our own hopes and dreams upon our children; instead, we need to seek God's will for their lives and encourage them to do the same. Let your children know from an early age that you are praying for them. Tell them you pray for their health, their callings, their future spouses, and anything else that comes to mind.

When your children begin to think seriously about their future callings, remind them you are there for them, you support them, and you are always available to talk. If they ask for your opinion, then you have an open door to share your heart with them. The goal is to create an atmosphere where you can express your thoughts without making your maturing children feel controlled. When they feel loved, heard, and understood, they are much more receptive to input. Should there be a decision you disagree with, you will have set the groundwork to discuss the matter lovingly and patience and without anger, frustration, or hurt.

Our number one responsibility as parents is to help lead our children to the saving grace of Jesus Christ. As soon as we find out we are pregnant, we want to begin praying for our babies. We pray that they will be healthy, grow strong in heart and character, and come to know Jesus as their Lord and Savior. When our babies are born, we continue these prayers, and we speak the grace and salvation that come only from a personal relationship with Jesus over their lives. Yes, they are only babies, but we can still speak the things of God over them.

> **Our number one responsibility as parents is to help lead our children to the saving grace of Jesus Christ.**

As our children grow up, we have the opportunity to talk to them about God and His love for us. We also begin to see their own unique traits—the special strengths, giftings, and characteristics that make them who God created them to be. During these seasons of growth, there are several ways we can be intentional about investing our love, time, and encouragement in our children.

FOCUS ON STRENGTHS

Spend time identifying your children's strengths, and remember that some strengths are more obvious than others. It's easy to spot a child who is good at sports or quick with his wit. The child who keeps her room and belongings organized is easy to recognize as someone who will succeed in detailed work. But what about the child who doesn't say much? Or the child who argues a lot? It's possible that what you see as a problem or a hindrance may actually be a strength needed for their future. For example, the quiet child may be a deep thinker who is extra perceptive and sensitive to the feelings of others. The child who seems to disagree with everyone may have the courage to make tough decisions when needed.

Here are four ways to identify strengths:

PRAY

Ask the Lord to show you your children's strengths. If you can't see these giftings right now, choose to trust that God knows your children even better than you do.

OBSERVE

What do your children like to do? What are the areas in which they excel? It could be any number or combination of things— art, music, academics, sports, problem solving, etc. As with all worthwhile investments, strengths require time and dedication to grow.

LISTEN

What do your children like to talk about? Whom do they look up to and why? When you intentionally spend time with and listen to your children, you will gain insight into their interests. This will give you an idea of their potential strengths, and you can help guide them in these areas. It's important to remember that supporting your children does not mean you cannot also be realistic. For example, they may want to do something that isn't compatible with your budget or your geographical area. That dream may need to wait. In the meantime, you and your children can pray together for God to either open the door to that opportunity or to redirect their hearts to a different interest.

ENCOURAGE

If you know me, then you know I love sports. Perhaps I should clarify—I love *watching* sports. When it comes to playing sports, the best place for me is on the sidelines (unless you count cornhole—sometimes I'm really good at that!). My point is that we don't have to be great at something to help our children be great. Both of my sons are gifted athletes. You're probably thinking, *You're their mother, so of course you think they're great.* Yes, I do, but it's also true. Jacob was a top-ranked high school tennis player in Texas, and he even tried his hand at a professional tennis career for a while. Joel was also a state-ranked tennis player, and he excelled in baseball too.

Even though I am not an athlete, I was still able to encourage and cheer for my athletic sons. When they chose to focus on other pursuits as they grew older, I continued to encourage and cheer for them. And although they are both grown and married now, I still make sure they know that I pray for them, believe in them, and will always be in their corner.

WORK THROUGH WEAKNESSES

In addition to strengths, every person has weaknesses. No one is good at *everything*. Many parents prefer to focus on their children's strengths, but it is also important to help them recognize their weaknesses and work through any issues.

Here are three common weaknesses to watch for and pray about in your children:

PRIDE

As your children grow in their strengths, they will probably be excited about their accomplishments. You will be too! Celebrate with them and encourage them to thank God for these strengths. It's tempting for us as humans to think, *I worked hard, so I deserve the attention and the credit.* However, that is pride. Pride takes the focus off God and puts it on us. The Bible warns us again and again about the dangers of pride, such as "Pride goes before destruction" (Proverbs 16:18) and "Pride ends in humiliation" (Proverbs 29:23).

Pride is such a sneaky and subtle trap that we often don't even realize we have fallen into it. If you sense some pride in your children's hearts, gently remind them that everything they have and all they are comes from God. He is the one who gives them their strengths, and He has a plan and a purpose for their lives. When they keep their focus on Him, the Lord will fulfill the dreams and desires of their hearts (Psalm 37:4).

FEAR

For some children, it can be overwhelming to hear that they have a special purpose in life. Perhaps someone has spoken a prophetic word over your child that one day he or she will speak in front of crowds of people. If your child is rather shy or prefers to be alone, then such a future can sound daunting and even scary.

Tell your children that God cares about their feelings. His plans for them are good and only good. Let them know that prophetic words are meant to bring encouragement and hope, not fear or confusion. No matter what, God will help your children and give them everything they need. They don't have to be afraid of the future because God will be with them every step of the way.

LAZINESS

If your children are old enough to walk, talk, and obey, then you have probably experienced the dreaded *laziness* struggle. Your precious, wonderful children (the ones who have so many strengths and terrific qualities) just can't seem to put their dirty clothes in the hamper, their dirty dishes in the sink, and their toys or belongings in their rooms. When you ask them to do something, you often hear one of these phrases:

- "I'll be right there."
- "I meant to do that yesterday."
- "I thought I already did that."
- "I forgot." (This was the most popular one in my house.)

What can you do to defeat laziness? Stand firm. Continue to remind and encourage your children to do what they need to do when they need to do it. It really is that simple. Help them understand your family's rules and expectations and, if necessary, set clear consequences for disobedience (more on that later in this chapter). It may take some trial and error, but your children will eventually get it.

One practical tip I often give parents is to make a chore list. For children who are too young to read, use pictures to show what needs to be done. For older children who can read, write out clear and simple directions. Commend them when they start doing their chores, and if something is challenging, encourage them to do their best. When the chores are complete, tell your children that you are so proud of them for listening and obeying.

SCHEDULE ONE-ON-ONE TIMES

Another intentional way to invest in your relationship with your children is to schedule one-on-one times with them. In my family, we called these special times "dates." These special times with each child allow you the opportunity to make fun memories with every member of your family.

- Allow your child to stay up later than usual so you two can share a favorite dessert or watch a favorite movie with popcorn.
- Have your child go grocery shopping or complete other errands with you and stop for a special treat on the way home.
- Pack some of your child's favorite foods and take him or her for a picnic lunch at the park.
- Invite your child to take a walk with you around the neighborhood. (For even more adventure, the two of you can run or exercise together. I never tried that with my sons, but I'm sure it's fun!)
- If your child is an avid reader, pick a book that both of you can read and discuss at a nearby coffee shop. (This is something that can be done over the course of a month or two.)

The frequency and nature of these one-on-one times will depend on the number of children you have, the flexibility of your budget, and the level of your energy. If you have an especially large family, there may be times when you want to invite two or three children to do something special. This can be a great time for the siblings to bond with each other as well as with you.

The way to make these special times a priority is to *schedule* them. Life gets so busy, and you don't want these sweet moments of uninterrupted connection to slip away. One-on-one times with your children will let them know that you enjoy being with them and will help create an environment for heart-to-heart talks.

DIFFERENT HOUSE, DIFFERENT RULES

When our sons were still young, Mike and I realized that every family has different rules when it comes to what language is appropriate, what television shows and movies are allowed, and what behaviors are acceptable. We explained to our sons that some families have rules similar to ours, while others may not. We also let them know that different doesn't necessarily mean wrong or bad—it's just different.

Mike and I came up with the phrase "different house, different rules." We wanted the boys to know that having different rules didn't necessarily mean we were right and everyone who chose to do something else was automatically wrong. When visiting another home, we emphasized the importance of honoring the rules of that home. We also told our sons that if they ever felt something was inappropriate or against our family rules, they could call us to discuss the situation.

As Christians, we all love God, but that doesn't mean we all have the same ideas about parenting. We can read the same Scriptures about parenting but still implement them differently. Does this mean some parents are better or holier than others? No, it means we each need to hear God for our own children. God will show you how to guide, teach, and direct your little ones. And because every child is unique, God will show you the best way to correct and connect with them. All you have to do is ask Him!

ENTERTAINMENT

> And now, dear brothers and sisters, one final thing. Fix your thoughts on what is true, and honorable, and right, and pure, and lovely, and admirable (Philippians 4:8).

Social media. Streaming services. Television shows and movies. There seems to be a never-ending supply of new content and new ideas that bring new ways to bombard our minds with all kinds of stuff, both good and not-so-good.

As parents, how can we protect our families? We start by praying about what we should and should not allow into our homes. The seemingly harmless things we may watch or listen to can leave behind a trail of ungodly thoughts, ideas, and images in our minds and in the minds of our children. It's up to us to be the gatekeepers and determine what is acceptable and what is not.

I have family and friends who choose not to have a television in their homes. I have other family and friends who have a television but watch it only sparingly. And I also have family and friends who watch television regularly. My point is that you don't have to be the same as anyone else. Ask the Lord, *What would You have our family do about the entertainment in our home?*

> **Ask the Lord, *What would You have our family do about the entertainment in our home?***

If your children are old enough to participate on social media sites and if you allow them to do so, then make it a priority to know what they are posting, what they are reading, and who they are following. You can also look at the sites and pages of your children's friends. *Isn't that an invasion of privacy?* you may wonder. Actually, it isn't. It's simply being a part of their world. Realistically, we may not be able to keep our children away from every inappropriate or negative thing, but by being aware of their online activities, you can help them avoid many potential pitfalls and painful situations.

Be diligent to secure safeguards on all computers, cell phones, and other electronic devices. Always let your children know that your desire is to keep them safe—not because you want to control them but because you love them. It's your job as a parent to help protect them from things that could be harmful to their body, soul, or spirit. Explain that anything that pulls their hearts away from you and God can keep them from His best for their lives.

LANGUAGE

What words and expressions are inappropriate for your family? These don't have to be limited to traditional curse words. There are many "slang" terms that you may choose to be off-limits as well. Be clear with your children about what is and is not acceptable. Remind them that other people (even Christians) may have different rules, but you as a parent are responsible to obey God's direction for your family. Also, this should go without saying, but I'll say it anyway—if our children aren't allowed to say certain words, we should set the example by not using those words ourselves.

FRIENDS

Who are your children's friends? What kind of impact do they have on your children? Perhaps you've never considered these questions. After all, one of the first things parents teach young children about social interactions is to play nicely with others. As children grow older, they begin to make friends through church, school, sports teams, and a variety of other avenues. An important part of being connected to your children's world is knowing about their friends, and the best way to find out is simply to ask questions like these:

- "Who are your friends at school?" (This question can be modified to include any location or activity.)
- "What do you and your friends like to do together?"
- "What interests do you share?"

Mike and I taught our sons to be thoughtful and wise about their closest friendships. We explained that they would be influenced by the people they spent the most time with, and this influence would either draw them closer to God or pull them away from Him.

Mike and I also made it a priority to get to know the parents of our sons' friends. You may think, *But I am too busy to add another thing to my schedule!* I really do understand, and I am not saying you have to hang out with everyone on a regular basis. Start by introducing yourself and exchanging phone numbers. If you are at an event for your children, try to sit together and get to know one another. Situations may arise in which you need to talk with those parents, and it benefits everyone to have laid a friendly foundation.

OBEDIENCE AND BLESSINGS

The Bible is the authority for all areas of life, and as parents, it's important to teach our children this truth. We want them to know that God's ways are always good and perfect, even when they seem contrary to what everyone else thinks. As we spend time reading God's Word to and with our children, they will learn how deeply they are loved and how trustworthy God really is. And when they ask, "Why should we obey what the Bible says?" we can explain that obedience brings God's protection and blessings.

Children need to know that obedience is not something we came up with to make them do (or not do) certain things. It's actually God's idea. In the same way, obedience is not about what we think is right or wrong but what God says is right or wrong. Here is what the apostle Paul wrote about this subject:

> Children, obey your parents in the Lord, for this is right. "Honor your father and mother"—which is the first commandment with a promise—"so that it may go well with you and that you may enjoy long life on the earth" (Ephesians 6:1–3 NIV).

Obedience is part of God's plan for our lives, and it's for our good. By the way, "our" refers to *everyone*. Our children need to know that everyone is under God's authority, and even adults are called to obedience. As parents, we must demonstrate that we are committed to the standards we set for our families. When there are inconsistencies between what we teach and what we actually say and do, our children will follow our example.

Obedience is a lifelong process that involves growing and maturing in our relationship with the Lord. We don't always do everything perfectly, and our children won't either. They may see, hear, say, or do something that is wrong, inappropriate, or sinful. When this happens, it is extremely important for our children to know they can come to us for help. We create this safe space by teaching them from an early age that they are loved unconditionally by God and by us and that nothing is too terrible to be forgiven. As they get older, we need to remind them often that they can tell us anything, and while there may be consequences (discussed in the following section), we will never reject them—no matter what.

DISCIPLINE, CORRECTION, AND CONSEQUENCES ... OH MY!

There are many books that focus on the intricacies of discipline, correction, and consequences. This isn't one of those books, but I would be remiss if I didn't at least address the topic.

I believe discipline is good. Why? Because God's Word says so.

> My child, don't reject the LORD's discipline,
> and don't be upset when he corrects you.
> For the LORD corrects those he loves,
> just as a father corrects a child in whom
> he delights (Proverbs 3:11–12).

The dictionary defines discipline as "training that corrects, molds, or perfects the mental faculties or moral character."[4] God disciplines us because we need to be corrected, molded, and perfected. He knows that this fallen world has all kinds of temptations and traps we can fall into, and He doesn't want us to suffer the consequences of sin. We may think of discipline as harsh or unfair, but it's actually God's way of protecting us and showing us how much He loves us.

Like God, we parents love our children. We want them to be obedient because we know obedience brings blessings. Ignoring disobedience does a genuine disservice to our children because it gives them the false belief that their actions have no consequences. Discipline is rarely pleasant or fun, but it shows our children we love them and want the best for their lives.

---

4. *Merriam-Webster.com Dictionary*, s.v. "discipline," accessed July 14, 2020, https://www.merriam-webster.com/dictionary/discipline.

Here are a few things to keep in mind on this subject:

SET EXPECTATIONS

Children need to know what behaviors are acceptable and what are not. They are very unlikely to meet your expectations if they don't know what those expectations are. And consequences without understanding create confusion and frustration.

From the time our sons were able to speak, Mike and I taught them to say "Please," "Thank you," "No, thank you," and "You're welcome." One of my sweetest memories is when I asked Jacob to do something and he politely replied, "No, thank you." Probably the nicest way of not doing what he was told to do!

We set the expectation for our sons to be polite and have good manners. We taught them how to act appropriately at the dinner table, how to shake hands when meeting someone new, and how to make eye contact when spoken to by others. Role playing at home helped our boys learn how to behave in public. This preparation was especially important during the years Mike played professional golf. Our family traveled for weeks and even months at a time, and wherever we went, our sons needed to know how to honor others through their words and actions.

When your children misbehave, address the issue as soon as possible (preferably the first time). Lovingly let them know their behavior is not acceptable. Tell them what the correct behavior looks like, what is expected in the future, and what the consequence will be for disobedience. You can also do some role playing to help them "see" the right thing to do in different situations.

Children who have been doing something for a while without correction often need to be reminded of your expectations. Be patient, make sure they understand what the correct behavior is, and answer any questions they have. Only you can determine when your children know what they are doing is wrong and a consequence is necessary. If your children are too young for such a discussion, you can still tell and show them what is and is not acceptable until they understand.

You may be surprised how quickly little ones can figure out what is and is not allowed. For example, when our sons were toddlers, Mike and I taught them that if they dropped (or threw) something from their highchairs, they would not get it back. They might be playing and toss a toy or food on the floor. Would we pick it up so they could do it again? After a bit of frustration and a few tears, our sons quickly learned the answer was no. This lesson was important for them to learn when we traveled as a family for Mike's career, because we ate at restaurants for two or three meals per day. Obedience made these meals much more pleasant for everyone, including the restaurant staff who appreciated not having to clean a bunch of food off the floor.

While it is important to correct your children when they misbehave, it's also important to recognize when they meet or even exceed your expectations. Make it a point to catch them doing something right. Perhaps you have asked your children to tidy up their rooms every evening before bedtime or to help young siblings with a chore. When you see them obeying or trying to be helpful, take a moment to acknowledge and celebrate them. Your affirmation is a great motivator for your children to keep doing the right thing.

BE CONSISTENT

My husband says, "Children don't do what we expect. They do what we accept." Once you set clear expectations for your children, you must be consistent in correcting any behaviors that are unacceptable. For example, you may have a child who yells whenever he gets frustrated or angry. If you set the expectation that yelling is not allowed in your family but only correct him every once in a while, then you send your child a confusing message. How will he know if yelling is acceptable or not?

> **Children don't do what we expect.
> They do what we accept.**

Children need consistency. They need to know what to expect from us. That being said, you don't have to do things exactly like other parents do. Ask the Lord to give you wisdom as to what kind of correction works best for your children. When my sons were young, I didn't want to tell them "no" every time they disobeyed. I thought it sounded negative and would lose its meaning if overused. Instead, I found that saying "You may not" was helpful and effective, and I sometimes followed up with, "That is a no."

FOLLOW THROUGH

When children disobey after knowing that such behavior is unacceptable, it is time to follow through with consequences. I'll admit that this is the hardest part of discipline. When you are in the middle of doing something else, it's inconvenient and often frustrating to have to stop and address the issue. It can be overwhelming when you have to correct multiple children every day, especially when you are already exhausted.

I really do understand. My sons were not perfect, and there were plenty of moments when I thought, *Not again!* However, I realized that as a parent, part of my obedience to the Lord was to teach my children right from wrong. If I failed to follow through with consequences, then I was teaching them a much different lesson—that disobedience is acceptable. This false belief would hurt their relationships not only with Mike and me but also with other human authority figures and with God. I chose to push through my discomfort, and the payoff was well worth it. We had a calmer, more peaceful home, and my sons grew up to be wonderful young men who love the Lord, love their families, and have great respect for authority.

Types of Consequences

What consequences are right for your children? That is a question only you and the Lord can answer. Here are some examples of possible consequences for young children:

- Time-outs
- Reduced or no screen time (television or other electronic devices)
- Loss of privileges (playdates, treats, special activities, etc.)
- Temporary loss of favorite toys or games

And here are some examples of possible consequences for older and young adult children:

- Loss of privileges (cell phone, car keys, computer, social activities, etc.)
- Additional chores
- Grounding (not being allowed to leave home except for school, church, or work)
- Apologizing and making things right with the offended person

These lists are not exhaustive, but they will give you a place to start. Younger children sometimes respond really well to simple things, such as a stern look or a firm voice. Other children require more tangible consequences.

Keep in mind that every child is different. A time-out may not be an effective deterrent for one child's disobedience, but for another child it could be just the thing to help him improve his behavior. There is also the possibility that one child might enjoy a time-out while a different child finds it devastating. For both children, this consequence has problems. It does nothing to discourage the first child's misbehavior, and it crushes the second child's spirit. Indifference and fear are two outcomes that need to be avoided when it comes to discipline. The best course of action is the one that helps children learn to do better next time and *want* to be obedient.

Some of you may be wondering, *What about spanking?* Yes, the Bible does mention this form of discipline. As with any other consequence, the best approach is to seek God's wisdom and guidance for your family.

Do consequences really work? Yes, they do. After a time or two, even a young child will understand that throwing toys at someone will result in not being allowed to play together. Older children will learn that disrespecting authority results in not being allowed to spend time with friends. And young adults will learn that breaking curfew results in not being allowed to drive the car (except for running errands for you, of course). As with any consequence, the best approach is to prayerfully seek God's heart, wisdom and guidance for each of your children."

All About the Heart

All discipline should be carried out with a large dose of love, patience, and kindness. These three factors will be the strongest motivators for our children to have obedient hearts in the future. That's right—it's all about the heart. When their hearts are aligned with ours, it will be much easier for them to do the right thing. Our children need to know we are for them, not against them. We are on the same team!

Discipline should never be done in anger. Please hear me out. I'm not saying anger itself is sinful or wrong. God gave us all of our emotions, and anger is a very normal reaction to pain, suffering, and injustice. The trouble with anger is that sometimes we can have a problem controlling it. We may do or say things we ordinarily wouldn't when we are angry, and then we have to deal with the fallout of our actions.

Consequences carried out in anger can create deep wounds in our children that last far longer than their unacceptable behaviors. Remember, the goal of discipline is to teach our children that obedience brings blessings to their lives. In tense times of correction, ask yourself, *Am I allowing God to direct my words and actions, or is anger controlling me?* Don't be afraid to step away for a moment, take a deep breath, and ask the Holy Spirit to bring peace to your heart and mind.

> **Consequences carried out in anger can create deep wounds in our children that last far longer than their unacceptable behaviors.**

When children are young, they obey because they don't want to experience the consequences that come with disobedience. There is nothing wrong with that. Even as adults, we obey rules and laws because we know there are consequences for not doing so, such as getting a ticket for driving faster than the speed limit. As our children get older, they discover that obedience does more than help them avoid consequences—it brings blessings to their lives.

93

When older children misbehave, ask them, "What does God think about this situation? What does His Word say about it?" Together, search the Scriptures to find out. The Bible addresses all kinds of behaviors and attitudes, and it's important for your children to see this for themselves. When our sons had disagreements with each other, Mike and I asked them, "Who will be the redeemer?" In other words, who will lay down their desires for the good of the relationship? Who will choose to make things right instead of having to be right? Now, our sons did not always work things out easily or quickly. They did not always choose to be a redeemer, but these questions helped lay a good foundation for dealing with conflict in relationships in the right way.

Prayer and Affirmation

I thank my God every time I remember you. In all my prayers for all of you, I always pray with joy (Philippians 1:3–4).

Make it a habit to end each time of discipline or consequences by praying out loud with your children. Thank God for the blessing they are to you and your family. Thank Him that they are growing in obedience and love every day. As you read this, you may think, *That sounds nice, but my children don't seem to be growing in either of those areas!* Even if your children aren't showing any signs of growth, your prayers are spoken prophetically—they declare what you are believing for the future. Your life-giving words will make a lasting imprint on your children's minds and hearts.

- For the child who struggles with sharing, thank God for her generous hands.
- For the child who argues and fights with his siblings, thank God for his loving and kind nature.

- For the child who is constantly in a bad mood, thank God for her joyful spirit.
- For the child who has only one level of noise (LOUD!), thank God for his calm and peaceful voice.
- For the child who obeys only when she feels like it, thank God for her obedient heart.

Speak life over your children. These are not prayers of denial but prayers of hope and belief in God's faithfulness and perfect timing.

FINAL THOUGHTS ON DISCIPLINE

No discipline is enjoyable while it is happening—it's painful! But afterward there will be a peaceful harvest of right living for those who are trained in this way (Hebrews 12:11).

Children do not come with an instruction manual, but we have unlimited access to their Designer and Creator. Ask the Lord to show you the best way to help each of your children learn the importance of obedience. Seek His heart regarding discipline and remember that different children and different situations may require different consequences.

Children need to know that you are serious about their obedience and that God is serious about it too. Consequences, though sometimes frustrating for everyone, will help them remember the rules. The ultimate goal is for your children to do the right thing because it's the right thing to do. They will make mistakes along the way, and in those moments, you will have to be patient and consistent. Let them know that nothing will change your love for them, and it is because you love them that you want to help them. With consistent guidance and encouragement, your children will learn to obey cheerfully and without complaint. And as I mentioned before, when you catch them doing something right, celebrate!

///////

Several years ago, I was preparing my notes for a parenting class at our church. I asked Jacob, who was engaged at the time, to tell me one thing that stood out about how I parented. He struggled at first, and I grew nervous. Then he said it was hard to come up with just one thing. (Whew!) So I said, "Well, give me three!" He replied, "Accountability, availability, and authority." As I thought about these three words, I realized they actually describe the process of intentionally investing in our children.

1. **Accountability**

   We are accountable to the Lord for parenting our children according to His Word. We teach them to succeed by seeking the Lord for wisdom and discernment, and in doing so, we help them recognize their God-given strengths and giftings.

2. **Availability**

   We represent the heart of the Father to our children until they are able to understand the Father's heart for themselves. God is always there for us, and part of our calling as parents is to be available to our children—to invest continually in their lives and to help them walk in obedience.

3. **Authority**

   We have a God-given authority to love our children and train them up in the way they should go. We do this by instilling spiritual truths and sharing our love for God's Word. As our children mature, they learn that all authority belongs to God. Obedience brings honor to Him and blessings to us.

Everything we do for and with our children is an investment of love being deposited into their hearts. These deposits will yield the wonderful return of growing relationships with us and with the Lord.

> **Everything we do for and with our children is an investment of love being deposited into their hearts.**

CHAPTER 5

STUDY GUIDE

REVIEW

We intentionally invest in our children as we help them grow in their strengths and work through their weaknesses. When we ask for His help, the Lord will give us wisdom regarding the rules and standards for our families. Discipline can be difficult at times, but it shows our children that we love them and want the best for them. As our children get older, they discover that obedience does more than help them avoid consequences—it brings God's blessings in their lives.

SCRIPTURES

- Deuteronomy 28:1–10
- Psalm 19:7–11
- Philippians 4:6–8
- Hebrews 12:5–11

QUESTIONS

- What strengths do you see in your children? How can you help them grow in these areas?
- What are your family's rules regarding entertainment and language?
- Why is consistency such a key part of discipline? How can you encourage your children when they make mistakes?

HEART CONNECTORS

- Schedule one-on-one time to pray with each of your children every week. (This special time is separate from bedtime prayers.) Praying out loud together may be new for you and your child, but just get started and the Lord will lead you both. Begin by thanking God for each other and for your family. Then pray about anything that comes to mind.

- Ask your children, "If you could be anything in the world, what would it be and why?" Write down their answers. Ask the same question again every few months to see if their answers change or if they still feel the same way. You will gain insight into the desires of their hearts and better understand how to pray for them and their future.

PRAYER

Father God, thank You for the wonderful plans You have for my children. Show me how to help them grow in their strengths and, more importantly, grow in their love for You. Your Word is the authority for our family, and we will not compromise our standards. Please give me wisdom and patience regarding discipline. I pray my children will always know they are loved, no matter what. Thank You for blessing and protecting them as they develop obedient hearts. In Jesus' name, Amen.

CHAPTER 6

STAY STRONG

Then Jesus said, "Come to me, all of you who are weary and carry heavy burdens, and I will give you rest. Take my yoke upon you. Let me teach you, because I am humble and gentle at heart, and you will find rest for your souls. For my yoke is easy to bear, and the burden I give you is light."

—Matthew 11:28–30

Motherhood is both beautiful and challenging. There are days when you feel as if you have everything under control. The baby is fed and sleeping peacefully. The toddler is playing quietly with his toys, and the older children are doing their chores and getting along wonderfully. Then there are other days. The baby is fussy and refusing to sleep. The toddler is throwing a tantrum because you won't let him color on the walls. And the older children? Well, let's just say they aren't cooperating with you or each other.

When my older son, Jacob, was born, I felt overwhelmed sometimes by the enormous responsibility of motherhood. I remember thinking, "He won't be fed, clean, held, or comforted if I don't do those things when they need to be done." Please don't misunderstand. I loved the baby stage, and I have loved every other stage from toddlerhood to adulthood too. Still, whether you have one child or many children, there are days that feel long and require more than your limited energy.

How do we make it through those tiring days? We rely on God's grace, strength, wisdom, and faithfulness. In Matthew

19:26, Jesus says, "With God everything is possible." It doesn't say everything will always be easy (as much as we might hope otherwise), but everything is *possible*. God loves you, and He loves your children. He will help you and give you everything you need to do what seems impossible.

TRUST

Trust in the LORD with all your heart;
> do not depend on your own understanding.
Seek his will in all you do,
> and he will show you which path to take
> (Proverbs 3:5–6).

We can trust the Lord to give us strength for each new day. He will show us unique ways of loving and parenting our children. Every single thing we do to train our children and every rule and consequence we put in place should serve to draw their hearts into a closer relationship with us and, ultimately, with God. He loves our children even more than we do, and He wants to walk with them all the days of their lives.

THANKFULNESS

Enter his gates with thanksgiving;
> go into his courts with praise.
> Give thanks to him and praise his name (Psalm 100:4).

When we acknowledge the greatness of God, we really can't help but praise Him and give Him thanks. Years ago, I decided to end every day with a "Top 10" thank you list for the Lord. Now, I admit there are times when I fall asleep before making the list, and sometimes I fall asleep in the middle of the list. However, the desire of my heart is for my final words and thoughts each night to be full of gratitude. I believe this practice blesses my heavenly Father, and it also makes me more aware of what He does for me throughout the day.

Most nights I have more than 10 things on my list, but every once in a while, I find myself stuck at seven or eight. Surely I have more to be thankful for, right? On those rare occasions I mentally replay my day in slow motion. I think about what I've done, whom I've spoken to, who reached out with an encouraging word, and what made me smile. Things that may have seemed commonplace at the time become "Top 10" items when brought to the forefront of my mind. Maybe I received a text from one of my sons or a friend I haven't seen for a while. Maybe one of my daughters-in-love invited me to spend the day with her, or perhaps I found special journal notes I had forgotten that I wrote years ago. (Some of those notes are in this book!) Maybe my husband surprised me with a romantic date night or did something sweet and thoughtful. Mike does make me a great cup of coffee just about every morning. I don't think I've ever put that on my list, but I should because I'm so thankful for his love and care.

Developing a thankful heart begins with being grateful for the things we might consider normal or mundane. These are the things that make life *our* life. They make us who we are. The simple patterns and rhythms of daily living are things to be treasured. Motherhood is full of routine and everyday occurrences, but we can have thankful hearts—not in spite of them but because of them.

> Motherhood is full of routine and everyday occurrences, but we can have thankful hearts—not in spite of them but because of them.

My daily thank you list keeps my heart focused on what's really important. The first five items are always the same:

1. My Lord and Savior, Jesus, who died on the cross for my sins
2. My husband, Michael
3. My children—our first baby, Jacob and Neeli (and Poppy, their baby girl in heaven), Joel and Danny, Jared, and Danielle
4. My parents
5. My dad and his good health

Before writing these top five things down on paper for this book, I never realized they were all about people. It makes sense, though, because when it comes down to what matters most, it is the people we love who make our lives rich and fulfilling.

Items 6–10 on my list change from day to day. They often include the small things that bring joy to my world, such as a beautiful sunset, an organized closet, or an unexpected phone call from a friend. Making this list opens my eyes to the many ways God shows me His love every day. I am richer for having this discipline in my life. Being intentionally thankful has taught me to treasure the people and the moments that make up my life.

It is in the sacred moments of thanksgiving that we find ourselves in God's presence. Psalm 100:4–5 tells us,

> Enter with the password: "Thank you!"
>> Make yourselves at home, talking praise.
>> Thank him. Worship him.
> For GOD is sheer beauty,
>> all-generous in love,
>> loyal always and ever (MSG).

When you give thanks and praise to God, your life will change. Your circumstances may appear the same, but your heart will have a new outlook based on His peace, love, and direction.

FAITHFULNESS

For the LORD is good.
His unfailing love continues forever,
and his faithfulness continues to each generation
(Psalm 100:5).

We can trust God because He is faithful. Our circumstances may seem impossible, but God is in control, and He will always have the last word. Does this mean life will always go our way? No, it means that despite what we see, God is always working on our behalf.

When the people of Israel fled from Egypt, they thought their long, hard days of suffering were over. They were finally free after centuries of slavery. Nothing could stop them now ... except the mighty Red Sea in front of them and the powerful Egyptian army behind them. How were they going to make it to the other side?

When the Red Sed saw you, O God,
its waters looked and trembled!
The sea quaked to its very depths.
The clouds poured down rain;
the thunder rumbled in the sky.
Your arrows of lightning flashed.
Your thunder roared from the whirlwind;
the lightning lit up the world!
The earth trembled and shook.
Your road led through the sea,
your pathway through the mighty waters—
a pathway no one knew was there! (Psalm 77:16–19).

"A pathway no one knew was there!" There will be times when you find yourself heading toward the unknown. Your marriage may be struggling, your finances may be tight, or your mind may be battling fear and anxiety. Perhaps you have a child who is sick, or you have troubling health issues of our own. Whatever the case may be, there's help and hope. God is with you in the battle. The way He chooses to bring you out of the war zone is up to Him—you may receive an "in the moment" miracle, or you may have a long journey to recovery. Either way, God will be with you through it all the way. When you think there's nowhere to go and the dim light at the end of the tunnel has faded away, He will be your Light. He will show you "a pathway no one knew was there." Whether this pathway is one of healing, restoration, or guidance, it will bring you to the heart of God. It will guide you to the place of knowing that your heavenly Father loves you, takes care of you, and is always faithful to you, even when you don't understand.

> **God is with you in the battle.**

In Chapter 4, I shared the story of when our son Joel had to have an MRI for a suspicious-looking spot on his hip. Knowing the situation could be serious, I prayed like I'd never prayed before. Morning, noon, and night, I knelt with my face to the ground and cried out to God to heal our son. The doctor called several days later with the incredible news that the spot, which he had thought to be cancerous, was gone. He said it was a miracle. God healed our son. All glory and honor to Him!

A few years later, our family needed another miracle. I was pregnant with Dani, and the doctors had given us one bad report after another. I prayed hard for my baby girl, just as I did for my son. After Dani was born, the prayers continued as we believed for God to heal her little body. After all, why wouldn't He? He'd done it before with Joel, and I knew He could do it again. Things turned out differently, however. Dani passed away a couple of months after her birth. My prayers were just as fervent, but the outcome was not the same.

I have to confess there were many questions in my mind and heart. *Why didn't my prayers work this time? Did I do something wrong? Did I pray wrong? Was my faith not strong enough?* I was confident that God could heal Dani just like He healed Joel, so why didn't He? I finally settled on the best answer I could—*I don't know why.* I don't know why Dani wasn't healed. I don't know why she died so soon. But what I do know is God cares for me and my family. I know He sent His Son, Jesus, to pay the price for my sins so I can live with Him forever in heaven. I know He gave me the strength to make it through that season of grief. I know, beyond any doubt, He loves me.

My prayers did not fall on deaf ears. I know God heard every one of them, and I am thankful we were able to hold Dani and be with her, even for that short time. Soon after she passed away, I asked the Lord, "Why did You let me have her if You knew she would leave us so soon?" In my heart I heard Him say, "Because I knew how much you loved her." What a sweet, amazing gift. I had the honor of loving our baby girl on earth, and she truly changed me. I suffered losses both before and after Dani, but her life is a constant reminder of God's love and faithfulness.

As long as we are on this earth, we are going to experience difficult things. There's no getting around it. However, God is always there to help us. The apostle Paul wrote,

Don't worry about anything; instead, pray about every-thing. Tell God what you need, and thank him for all he has done. Then you will experience God's peace, which exceeds anything we can understand. His peace will guard your hearts and minds as you live in Christ Jesus (Philippians 4:6–7).

God is faithful. He will carry us when we can't take another step, strengthen us when we are weak, and give us peace when our hearts are in turmoil. He will show us "a pathway no one knew was there."

WALKING THROUGH FIRE

When you go through deep waters,
    I will be with you.
When you go through rivers of difficulty,
    you will not drown.
When you walk through the fire of oppression,
    you will not be burned up;
the flames will not consume you (Isaiah 43:2).

Everyone has their own story that reveals where their heart intersected with God's heart. My story is about faith—believing in who God *is* and not solely in what He *does*. Some people might say I got my miracle when God healed Joel, and that is true. However, I got a miracle with Dani too. It just didn't look the way I thought it would. Instead of healing for my baby girl's body, I received God's healing for my broken heart.

From beginning to end, the Bible is filled with amazing, true stories of God's faithfulness. God rescued Noah, his family, and two of every kind of animal from the flood that covered the entire earth. God used Moses to deliver the Israelites from slavery in Egypt and led them to the Promised Land. God kept His promise to send a Messiah to save His people, and Mary miraculously conceived and gave birth to Jesus.

There are many such stories that minister to my heart, but one of my favorites is the story of Shadrach, Meshach, and

Abednego in Daniel 3. After King Nebuchadnezzar conquered Jerusalem, these three young men were taken to Babylon as captives. They impressed the king with their wisdom and judgment and eventually received positions of authority. One day King Nebuchadnezzar set up a giant golden statue and ordered everyone in his kingdom to bow down and worship it. He declared, "Anyone who refuses to obey will immediately be thrown into a blazing furnace" (v. 6).

Shadrach, Meshach, and Abednego did not obey this command, and the king was furious. When he repeated his threat to throw them into the furnace, the three men replied:

> O Nebuchadnezzar, we do not need to defend ourselves before you. If we are thrown into the blazing furnace, the God whom we serve is able to save us. He will rescue us from your power, Your Majesty. But even if he doesn't, we want to make it clear to you, Your Majesty, that we will never serve your gods or worship the gold statue you have set up (vv. 16–18).

Outraged at their response, King Nebuchadnezzar ordered his servants to increase the furnace's heat to seven times its normal level. Shadrach, Meshach, and Abednego were tied up and thrown inside. The furnace was so hot that the soldiers who threw them in died from the flames.

When the king looked inside the furnace, he couldn't believe his eyes. Not only were the three men untied and unharmed, but there was also a fourth man inside who "looks like a god!" (v. 25). King Nebuchadnezzar immediately called Shadrach, Meshach, and Abednego to come out of the furnace. Verse 27 says, "The fire had not touched them. Not a hair on their heads was singed, and their clothing was not scorched. They didn't even smell of smoke!" The king couldn't help but praise God:

Praise to the God of Shadrach, Meshach, and Abednego! He sent his angel to rescue his servants who trusted in him. They defied the king's command and were willing to die rather than serve or worship any god except their own God.... There is no other god who can rescue like this! (vv. 28–29).

Shadrach, Meshach, and Abednego refused to allow their circumstances, and even the threat of death, to shake their trust in God. They knew He could miraculously save them from the furnace, but they also choose to be faithful "even if he doesn't" (v. 18). Moments such as these define our faith. It doesn't mean we are not allowed to feel confused, sad, or even mad, but rather that we believe God is in control, He has a plan, and He "causes everything to work together for the good of those who love God and are called according to his purpose for them" (Romans 8:28).

Was I sad when we miscarried our first baby, when we lost Jared, and when Dani died? Yes. Was I confused? Yes. Was I mad? No, I never got mad. I don't believe it would have been wrong or sinful to be mad, but I didn't feel that way. I just wondered why some children survive while others do not. I still don't understand that, but I know that I know that God has a plan. I have learned to trust Him with my happy moments and with my heartbreaking times as well. He is a God of miracles, and He can be trusted even when things don't go as we may like.

> He is a God of miracles, and He can be trusted even when things don't go as we may like.

UNTOUCHED BY FLAMES

One of the most incredible parts of the story of Shadrach, Meshach, and Abednego is that there was no trace of smoke on them. If you've ever been around any kind of fire (even a campfire), then you know the smell of smoke permeates *everything*—clothes, hair, the inside of your nose, etc. So why was there no smell of smoke on these three men? Because the Lord was with them in the furnace. He completely protected them from the effects of the fire.

Have you ever been through a fire? Perhaps not literal flames but a really difficult time or situation when you felt there was no way out? We've all experienced hurt or pain in some way. The Lord wants you to know He is there for you. He will walk with you through every fire. There may be a miracle in the making even now, and if so, praise God! Or things may not go as you hope. Still, praise God. Praise Him because He is with you in every moment of every situation you face. He is with you in the heat of your battles, and regardless of the outcome, you can come through without a hint of smoke.

This verse is so encouraging to me:

But all who listen to me will live in peace,
    untroubled by fear of harm (Proverbs 1:33).

Notice that it doesn't say we won't ever have fear or suffer harm. Instead, when we do experience them, we will be "untroubled." Despite our circumstances, we can live in peace because we belong to the Lord.

Dani's short, precious life helped me grow in my ability to trust God in the "even if he doesn't" circumstances. We will not always understand everything that happens this side of heaven, but I can assure you from firsthand experience that

God's faithfulness is all-encompassing and never-ending. He loves us, He sees us, and He will carry us through our toughest times. He is good. He can be trusted.

SEEKING GOD ABOVE ALL

Seek the Kingdom of God above all else, and live righteously, and he will give you everything you need (Matthew 6:33).

God's wisdom, love, strength and help are available to all His children all the time. We have direct access to the heart of our Father through worship, prayer, and His Word. Every time you read the Bible, the Lord will show you something new, or He will reinforce what He has shown you before.

How can you know that you are seeking God first and making Him your number one priority? Ask yourself these questions:

- Where do I spend most of my time and energy?
- Do I ask God first before making decisions?
- Do I really see His Word as the ultimate truth for my life?

Only you can determine the nature of your relationship with the Lord and where He stands on your list of priorities. Here are some things you can do to help make Him the most important thing in your life.

BE BIBLE-READY

Keep an open Bible where you will see it throughout the day. You can read some Scripture whenever you have a few minutes here and there. It might work well on your kitchen counter or on a shelf in your laundry room. The bathroom is also a good place since you will be in there at some point during your day.

Additionally, carry a Bible or devotional in your purse or diaper bag so you can read during free moments when you are out and about.

Take advantage of naptime. When your children are sleeping, resist the urge to reach for your to-do list or clean the house. Spend some time with the Lord. When we practice being like Mary, who sat at the feet of Jesus (see Luke 10:39), I believe God will bless our time and help accomplish everything we need to do.

Babies often seem to sleep better during the day than at night. Make the most of those 2 am wake-up calls. As you feed, change, or rock your little one, listen to the Bible on your phone. There are multiple free Bible apps, including YouVersion Bible, Bible Gateway, and Logos Bible Study Tools. Sometimes toddlers wake up in the middle of the night too. Try reading a little from the Bible as you settle them back to sleep.

Be intentional about meditating on God's Word. If you can't spend long periods of time reading your Bible, then choose two or three verses to memorize every week. Write these verses on index cards that you can put around the house (on the bathroom mirror, near the kitchen sink, etc.) or even make them your background on your phone or computer. When I was pregnant with Jacob, the first thing I learned by heart was Psalm 23. I knew that as a new mom I might have long and tiring days, and memorizing Scripture made it easier to get in God's Word regularly.

Ask God to help you make His Word a reality in your daily life. He understands that young children need your constant attention, and He also knows that older children need your consistent encouragement and counsel. God will show you unique ways to grow in your faith in each season. Remember, you are His beloved daughter. He loves you, and He will refresh you in your calling as a mom.

PRAY AND PRAISE

As with Bible reading, your prayer time may happen in the middle of the night as you tend to your baby. When you have toddlers running around, you can pray during naps or bathroom breaks. (Sometimes it seems that even getting a bathroom break is an answer to prayer!) You can also talk to God outside. On days when the weather is nice, put your little one in a stroller and take a walk around the block. It will do you (and your child) good to get sunshine, fresh air, and exercise as you pour out your heart to God.

Any place and time is a good place and time to call on the name of the Lord. It's also good for your children to see and hear you praying. If there is something specific on your mind, such as a family member who is sick or a friend who is having financial problems, let your children know and ask them to join you in prayer. You don't have to give them all the details—just share what you feel is appropriate for their level of understanding. Pray out loud and ask if they'd like to pray too. As your children grow older, they will become more and more comfortable praying for others because they will have learned from your example.

> **Any place and time is a good place and time to call on the name of the Lord.**

Let praise fill the air of your home. When you're cleaning, cooking, or playing with the children, play music that glorifies God. Praise and worship changes the atmosphere around you— it drives irritations, bad attitudes, and lies from the enemy away and replaces them with joy and harmony. My children are grown and married now, but I still enjoy playing praise and worship in the house, especially when Mike and I have visitors. It sets the peaceful atmosphere we want to have for our family and guests. I also play praise and worship music in the car. Wherever I go, I want the presence of God to go with me!

Prayer, praise, and God's Word strengthen us. These three things give us the spiritual nourishment we need every day. It is wonderful to have godly family and friends we can ask for help, but it would be foolish to forget the Lord. He should be the One we run to first, not our last resort.

KEEP THE SABBATH

What is the Sabbath? Why is it important? In Exodus 20, God gives His people the Ten Commandments, and the fourth commandment is all about the Sabbath.

> Remember to observe the Sabbath day by keeping it holy. You have six days each week for your ordinary work, but the seventh day is a Sabbath day of rest dedicated to the LORD your God. On that day no one in your household may do any work.... For in six days the LORD made the heavens, the earth, the sea, and everything in them; but on the seventh day he rested. That is why the LORD blessed the Sabbath day and set it apart (vv. 8–11).

Here is a beautiful truth about the Sabbath: God made it for you! This weekly one-on-one time with your heavenly Father allows you to focus your attention on your relationship with Him. It also brings renewed strength to your body, soul, and spirit.

Another way to get refreshment and direction from the Lord is to have regular sabbaticals. A sabbatical is a time of rest, additional to the weekly Sabbath, and though its length is between you and the Lord, it usually lasts longer than one day. For me, rest might look like reading, journaling, and sipping a cup of tea in a quiet, relaxing place. Depending on your budget and any other restraints, you can have this uninterrupted time wherever you would like. You may enjoy your sabbatical at an out-of-town location or in the lobby of a beautiful nearby hotel.

If you're a single mom with young children, consider hiring a babysitter for an afternoon or evening. If that's not doable, then ask a close friend or trusted family member to watch the children for a few hours. You can also have someone watch your little ones while you take some alone time in your bedroom. Even if none of these options work for you, please know that the Lord will meet with you after the children are asleep for the night. Grab some tea, your Bible, and your journal and sit in the most comfortable place in your home. Enter His presence with prayers of praise and thanksgiving, and enjoy this time with the Lord. This is something we all can do on a regular basis.

While these special times with the Lord are great for us as individuals, they are also wonderful for husbands and wives to experience together. Prayers, discussions, and times of quiet with each other and the Lord will help you both listen to what He wants to say regarding yourselves, your marriage, and your parenting.

Jesus often went away from the crowds to be alone with the Father (see Luke 5:16). He knew the importance of spending time in God's presence, and He set this example for us. God loves you and wants to speak to your heart about the things that matter to you and the things that matter to Him. Prayerfully seek God's heart for what a Sabbath and a sabbatical look like for you and your family.

A MOM LIFE SCRIPTURE

Years ago, I read a Scripture that really spoke to my heart as a mom, and it immediately became my life Scripture for mother-hood.

> Rejoice always, pray continually, give thanks in all circum-stances; for this is God's will for you in Christ Jesus (1 Thessalonians 5:16–18 NIV).

Have joy in everything. Pray about everything. Give thanks in everything. For me this Scripture sums up what being Mom is all about. It is a constant reminder to go to the Father for every single thing. He is always available to help us, encourage us, and guide us. He does all this and more because He loves us. Don't be discouraged if there is an area of weakness in your life. We are all in the process of learning, growing, and healing. Go to the Father and ask Him to help you.

PERFECTLY LOVED

You may wonder why I keep focusing on the importance of reading the Bible, praying, and learning to hear God's voice. Will He love you more if you do these things? Actually, no. God can't love you *more* because He already loves you fully, completely, and eternally. You can, however, grow in your understanding of His love. Spending time in God's presence will help you become more aware of who He is and how much He cares about every aspect of your life. You are perfectly loved by your heavenly Father, and when you realize this, your love for Him will grow in return.

Spending time in God's presence will help you become more aware of who He is and how much He cares about every aspect of your life.

Hang in there, mom. Don't give up. Stay strong! You've got this because God's got you, and He will never let you go.

CHAPTER 6

STUDY GUIDE

REVIEW

We can trust the Lord to give us strength, wisdom, and grace for even the most challenging days of motherhood. Developing a heart of gratitude helps us remember His unfailing love and faithfulness, and when we walk through the fires of life, we can praise Him regardless of the outcome. God is available to help us every moment of every day. As we honor Him with our time and attention throughout our busy schedules, He will refresh us in our callings as moms.

SCRIPTURE READING

- Joshua 1:9
- Psalm 23
- Psalm 136
- Ephesians 6:10–19

QUESTIONS

- What are some small things that bring joy to your world?
- In what area(s) of your life do you need God to make "a pathway no one knew was there"?
- When are some times during the day (or night) that you can spend a few moments alone with God? What would your ideal sabbatical look like?

HEART CONNECTORS

- Make it a daily habit to thank God for 10 things and keep these lists in your journal. Ask your children to make "Top 10" lists as well. (For young children, a shorter list is perfectly fine. The point is to help them learn about gratitude). Schedule a day and time to share your lists as a family. If your children are older and out of the house, then share your lists when you visit or during phone calls.

- Ask the Lord to give you a Scripture of encouragement as a mom. In addition to writing it in your journal, write it on an index card or piece of paper and put it where you can see it every day. It will serve as a reminder that what you do as a mom matters. You can also help your children find a favorite Scripture for themselves. Have them write it down and keep it in their Bibles.

PRAYER

Father God, thank You for being with me on both the beautiful days and the challenging days of motherhood. You are so faithful to provide exactly what I need, often before I realize I need it! I believe You are by my side through every situation. I choose to trust You even when I don't understand the outcome, because I know You are good. Please show me how to grow in my faith and make time with You a priority every day. In Jesus' name, Amen.

CHAPTER 7

TWO BECOME ONE

So the LORD God caused the man to fall into a deep sleep. While the man slept, the LORD God took out one of the man's ribs and closed up the opening. Then the LORD God made a woman from the rib, and he brought her to the man.
"At last!" the man exclaimed.
"This one is bone from my bone,
and flesh from my flesh!
She will be called 'woman,'
because she was taken from 'man.'"
This explains why a man leaves his father and mother and is joined to his wife, and the two are united into one.
                                        —Genesis 2:21–24

This chapter is directed primarily toward married moms, but if you are single, please don't feel left out or skip ahead. I truly believe there is something for everyone in the following pages. For the mom who wants to be married someday, tuck these truths inside your heart and ask God to help you prepare to be the best wife you can be. For the mom who doesn't see marriage in her future, still take these truths to heart and ask God to show you how you can grow in your relationship with Him. Every mom, single or married, is loved by our heavenly Father, who delights in blessing His daughters.

////////

Mike and I surrendered our lives to the Lord just over a year after we were married. Recognizing the importance of what He had to say about marriage and family (as well as everything else), we made the decision to read the Bible and make it our handbook for doing life. Another thing Mike brought up several times during those early years was the idea of attending a marriage conference. I told him we didn't need to attend any kind of marriage training, whether it be a conference, class, or seminar, because we weren't one of those couples who have problems. Mike would let it go for a while, but then he'd bring up the idea again. I continued to hold my position that we didn't need help. We were good. The truth is I thought those marriage events were for couples who were struggling in their relationships, and I didn't want to be put into that category. What would people think? I was more concerned about other people's opinions than my husband's desires, and I was wrong. I just didn't know it yet.

It took me 10 years to lay down my pride and agree to go. We had moved back to Texas and started attending Gateway Church, where there was going to be a marriage seminar with Pastor Jimmy Evans. Mike asked if we could go, and this time I said yes. It was one of my best decisions ever. You might think I am exaggerating, but that seminar truly changed my life and our marriage. I still remember going to lunch during the break and just talking and talking with my sweet husband. We shared our hearts, joys, hurts, and goals, and we reaffirmed our love for each other. That day stands out as one of the most pivotal moments in our married life. Since then, we have attended Pastor Jimmy's marriage event, now called the XO Conference, every year. Mike later served as a marriage pastor at Gateway Church, and during that season, we sometimes attended even more than once a year. Each time, we walked away feeling encouraged and excited for our future together.

Your marriage is worth the effort to do whatever you can to make it better and stronger year after year. God wants your marriage to succeed and reflect His love, which is always faithful and endlessly enduring.

MARRIAGE AND PARENTING

Why do I have a chapter on marriage in a book about motherhood? Because I believe a solid marriage is the best foundation for parenting. The way to build this firm foundation is to follow what God has to say about the relationship between husbands and wives. The heart connection you have with your children improves when you make your marriage a priority. The stronger your marriage, the better your parenting.

> The stronger your marriage, the better your parenting.

When I was in elementary school, we used to play Red Rover. Do you remember that game? Children divided into two teams and faced each other in lines several yards apart. Team A formed a chain by holding hands and called to Team B, "Red Rover, Red Rover, let (insert name) come over." The person from Team B whose name was called then ran as fast as he or she could toward Team A and tried to break the chain by targeting the weakest link. I didn't really like this game very much. Because I was small and not very strong, I was often seen as the weakest link. Consequently, my hands and arms were a bit sore after this game. I did learn, though, that if my teammates and I held each other's hands tightly, stood firmly on the ground, and gave a bit when the person ran into us, we weren't going to break.

It might be a bit uncomfortable, but our chain would remain secure.

Many years later, I was married, born again, and preparing to teach a marriage class with my husband at our church. I was in the process of organizing our notes when I suddenly remembered Red Rover. I realized that the steps that helped me do well in the game could also help people do well in their marriages.

1. **Hold on—to the Lord and to each other.**
   It's important to hold on to the Lord first. When He is our anchor, it is easier to hold on to each other.
2. **Stand firm—planted in God's Word.**
   There are many resources that claim to be able to help couples through marital crises. We need to be sure that whatever (or whomever) we look to for help is grounded in God's Word. The Bible is true, unwavering, and full of life.
3. **Give a little (or a lot)—in humility.**
   When we humbly seek understanding and unity with each other, God brings revelation and peace, and we grow stronger and more resilient in our relationship. Is it okay to be upset? Yes. Is it okay to stay upset? No. If we aren't willing to work toward a resolution, then we will never get to a place of harmony.

Make allowance for each other's faults and forgive anyone who offends you. Remember, the LORD forgave you, so you must forgive others. Above all, clothe yourselves with love, which binds us all together in perfect harmony (Colossians 3:13–14).

Harmony. The word itself sounds nice, doesn't it? It means agreement, accord, and tranquility.[5] Don't we all want that

---

5. *Merriam-Webster.com Dictionary*, s.v. "harmony," accessed July 23, 2020, https://www.merriam-webster.com/dictionary/harmony.

for our marriages? Absolutely! Getting to a place of harmony may not always be easy, but the blessings it brings make it well worth the effort.

JOY GIVERS

Each new day gives us a fresh opportunity to bring joy into our marriages. To help you find renewed joy with your husband, I've compiled a list of what I call "Joy Givers." These are ideas and Scriptures that have truly transformed my relationship with Mike and brought unity and understanding into our daily lives as husband and wife. As you read through the list, you may find that you're hitting the mark on some or even most of the suggestions. If, however, you recognize some areas that need a boost, please don't feel bad. I know I keep saying this, but it is worth repeating—we are all learning and growing. Mike and I have been married for 30 years, and so far, neither of us has reached perfection. Talk to your husband about the areas in which you see room for improvement. Pray together and ask God to show you how to move forward as a team.

SHARE YOUR HEART EVERY DAY

When life gets busy, it's easy to allow distractions to get in the way of daily conversations with your husband. And by conversations, I mean talks that aren't always about the children. However, connection is a key component of healthy relationships, and an important way spouses connect is by talking and sharing their hearts with one another on a regular basis. After your children are in bed, spend time chatting about each other's day. If you find that one or both of you needs more time to talk, then schedule it. That's right—set aside a time and place for uninterrupted conversation. You may have to wake up a little earlier or go to bed a little later, but you will never regret connecting with each other's hearts.

COMMIT TO CHURCH

Let us think of ways to motivate one another to acts of love and good works. And let us not neglect our meeting together, as some people do, but encourage one another, especially now that the day of his return is drawing near (Hebrews 10:24–25).

Attending church services together (and with your children) demonstrates that obedience to God is a priority to your family. When you spend time with other believers who motivate you to grow in your faith, your relationship with the Lord strengthens, and that is always a blessing to your marriage. You can also find joy and connection with your husband by serving together at your church. Whether the two of you greet visitors, pray with people, or teach a class, you will find that encouraging others actually encourages you as a couple too.

You may wonder, *But what about online services?* Many churches do stream their services online, and I think that is wonderful, especially for anyone who is traveling, sick, or otherwise unable to attend in person. However, there is something unique and powerful about gathering with your brothers and sisters in Christ and corporately worshipping the Lord. If I am healthy and able to go to church, then I want to be there!

SCHEDULE REGULAR DATES

Think back to when you first fell in love with your husband. How fun was it to decide what to wear and how to fix your hair for your dates? Whether the two of you were going to a restaurant to eat dinner, the theater to see a movie, or somewhere else to enjoy a surprise outing, the anticipation for your special night was exciting.

Fast forward to the present. Are you still experiencing the exciting anticipation of date nights? If not, then it's time to start—right now! You may object, "But my children are too young to stay by themselves. We can't afford a babysitter, and the grandparents don't live nearby. Plus, I'm just too tired after a long day." I understand. Really, I do. I was a homeschool mom from the time my sons began kindergarten until the time they finished high school. I served in various ministries at our church, and I also had a small business for several years. Here's the thing, though: one-on-one time with your husband is important for the health of your relationship, and if you don't make it a priority, then it simply won't happen.

Getting ready for a date with your husband creates excitement as you look forward to spending time together. Dates don't have to be elaborate or expensive to be meaningful. They also don't have to be at night. Here are some fun, low-cost ideas for one-on-one time with your husband:

- Start the day by having breakfast together. If your children are early risers, this alone time may be short, but it can still be sweet.
- Play a game or put a puzzle together.
- Make (or buy) a special treat to share while watching a movie.
- Take a walk around your neighborhood or the local park.
- Explore a new coffee shop or bookstore.
- Learn something new. This can be anything from learning how to cook a new food to learning how to speak a new language.

One of the biggest hurdles to having a date with your husband can be finding someone to watch the children. You probably have friends who face the same challenge. If these friends are trustworthy, then a great solution might be a rotating schedule. You could watch their children one night every other week, and they could watch yours on the opposite weeks. Everyone gets two date nights per month!

PRAY TOGETHER

Prayer is one of the most intimate things you can do with your husband. This spiritual connection will draw your hearts closer to each other and to the Lord. Set aside some time each day to pray together. You may prefer to pray early in the morning or just before bed. You can also pray together over the phone or through video chat when one (or both) of you is out of the house. Remember, there is no right or wrong way to pray—it's simply talking to God.

If praying together is new to you, start with short and sweet prayers, such as:

- "Bless my husband."
- "Bless our marriage and our children."
- "Thank You, Lord, for this new day. Help us follow You in all that we do."
- "Please keep our family safe and healthy."
- "Help us bring Your joy and peace to the people we see throughout our day."

These are short prayers you can say every day and finish with "In Jesus' name, Amen." As you get more comfortable praying together, you can add anything that either of you would like to pray about (jobs, finances, children's needs, future plans, etc.). Before you know it, these sweet times will be something you look forward to every day.

COMMUNICATE YOUR NEEDS

Many wives say that what goes on outside the bedroom will add or subtract to what goes on inside the bedroom. After a long, draining day, they need a heart connection to relax and unwind. In other words, some women want to share their thoughts and emotions before they share their bodies.

It's different for most husbands—they tend to be able to compartmentalize much more easily than their wives. Men can have a rough day at work, not want to talk about it, and still be ready for sex later that evening. When a stressed wife says, "Let's go to bed," a husband may be surprised to learn that she isn't being flirtatious—she actually wants to go to sleep.

Of course, not all women are the same, and neither are all men. Sexual intimacy is a sacred and beautiful gift in marriage, and it requires open and honest communication. Tell your husband what you need and listen to what his needs are as well. It's not unusual for one spouse to have a greater desire for sex than the other, and this balance can shift based on many different variables. Be sensitive and serve one another in love, both in and out of the bedroom.

CHOOSE TO FORGIVE

Forgiving a friend, relative, or colleague who has hurt you can be difficult. Forgiving a spouse who has hurt you can be a lot more challenging. Why? Because we love our spouses the most and expect the most from them.

How do we move past the hurt and anger to a place of forgiveness? As Christians, we are called to forgive others just as Jesus forgave us. It's tempting to think, *Well, He's Jesus, the Son of God. He's perfect, so it's easy for Him to forgive.* The reason Jesus forgives us is because He loves us. Jesus suffered a horrible death on the cross and paid the price for our sins because He loves us. He offers us eternal life with Him in heaven because He loves us. Jesus' love for us is our example of forgiveness.

The apostle Paul wrote, "Be kind to each other, tenderhearted, forgiving one another, just as God through Christ has forgiven you" (Ephesians 4:32). Although this isn't a "marriage" verse, it still applies to the relationship between husbands and wives. Forgiveness is all about love. We forgive because we love Jesus. We forgive because we love our husbands. We forgive because we are called to love.

> **Forgiveness is all about love.**

I'm not saying forgiveness is always easy or comfortable. I'm not saying it will fix everything right away. If there is any type of abuse in your relationship, please reach out for help immediately. Seek counsel for the health and safety of everyone involved.

WORK THROUGH CONFLICT

Take a deep breath and repeat after me: "Conflict is not a bad word." I know it can feel scary, but disagreements and differing opinions are actually normal parts of a relationship. After all, you are two different people with distinct thoughts, feelings, needs, and desires. Conflict only becomes a problem when we see it as a personal win or lose scenario. You see, marriage is a joint effort. Either both spouses win, or both spouses lose.

How should you respond to conflict in your marriage? Work with your husband to find a solution to the issue at hand. Listening to each other makes it much easier to find common ground. Common ground doesn't necessarily mean equal, though. Sometimes one spouse has more responsibility in a certain situation and needs to take ownership of the problem before a solution can be found. When you humbly admit your mistakes, you take a crucial step toward resolving the issue, and that is a win-win for everyone.

I must confess that it isn't always easy for me to remain calm when I feel that I've been wronged or misunderstood. However, this is what the Bible says about anger:

Don't sin by letting anger control you.
Think about it overnight and remain silent (Psalm 4:4).

How can I "remain silent"? There's only one way—I have to take my anger and hurt to the Lord. When I let Him hold my heart, anger loses its control over me. Many times, after praying about something, I find there's no longer a need to discuss it with Mike. My heart is settled because I've sought the Lord through His Word and prayer. He helps me better understand the situation and shows me if I have some fault in it as well. Of course, there are times when I do need to address something with my husband. Our conversations are much more productive after I've taken a step back to pray, because I am calmer and able to better articulate what is bothering me.

Determine today that your home will be a safe place where you and your husband can be honest about anything and everything. Remind each other that you are a team. When one person struggles, you struggle together. Don't be embarrassed to ask for help if the conflict feels too difficult to handle on your own. There are wonderful Christian marriage counselors who can help you and your husband navigate complicated or sensitive issues. I also recommend finding a godly older couple who have a strong, healthy marriage and seeking their wisdom and advice.

Regardless of the levels of fault in any situation, Mike and I have learned the importance of repentance and forgiveness. Repent and forgive. Every time. No exceptions. We've determined that it's best for our marriage to focus on doing right, rather than being right.

LISTEN AND LEARN

Do you find it frustrating when you are talking to someone and you can tell their focus is anywhere but your conversation? Spouses feel that way too. When your husband talks to you, stop whatever else you are doing and give him your undivided attention. Saying "Uh huh" every now and then while doing something else is not listening. It's hearing. Hearing is done with our ears, but listening is done with our hearts. Lean in with your heart so you can be fully present and attentive to your husband. If he says something you don't fully understand, allow him to finish and then ask questions for clarification.

> **Hearing is done with our ears, but listening is done with our hearts.**

I realize undivided attention can be difficult to give when you have young children who need to be cared for and supervised. If you find yourself distracted, then be honest and say something like, "I really care about what you have to say, but I am struggling to focus at the moment. Can we please pause this conversation until the children are in bed so I can give you my full attention?"

When husbands and wives give each other the space needed to share their thoughts, they show respect and honor for one another. They may also discover things they never knew before. Likes, dislikes, opinions, and dreams can change over the years, and wise spouses make it a lifelong habit to listen and learn about each other.

SHARE YOUR VISION

Spend time talking, praying, and hearing God with your husband. I have friends who take a special trip called a "vision retreat" each year for this purpose. They may stay in a nearby hotel or go further away from home, but the point is to get away from life's normal distractions and focus solely on God and each other.

During our 30 years of marriage, Mike and I have gone on several vision retreats, but we have much more frequent "vision talks." About once a month, we talk about our thoughts, plans, and dreams for our marriage and family and for ourselves regarding ministry and personal goals. We pray and ask God for His wisdom and direction. This time is not scheduled; instead, it's an organic, ongoing conversation of where we are and where we want to go.

Whether you choose to have retreats, talks, or something else, be intentional to share and pray about what God is saying to you as individuals and as a couple. He has a beautiful plan for your marriage. Make time to hear it!

SPEAK LIFE

The next chapter in this book is about the importance of speaking life over your children. Speaking life over your husband matters just as much. *What* you say and *how* you say it will either bring your relationship closer together or drive it further apart. Make a conscious and continuous effort to speak words of encouragement over your husband and your marriage.

Speaking life is not about saying half-truths or ignoring issues. On the contrary, if there's a problem that needs addressing, by all means bring it up. Just do so with a large dose of kindness, gentleness, and love. When you choose to make life-giving words part of your daily conversations, you will

THE JOY OF BEING MOM

reap the benefits of having a marriage in which you and your husband can share your hearts openly and honestly.

By the way, *when* you say something it is just as significant as what you say and how you say it. If either or both of you have had a long day, or if time is limited, then it is likely best to wait and have important discussions about your marriage, the children, or any other subject at a different time.

SEEK GODLY FRIENDSHIPS

As iron sharpens iron,
    so a friend sharpens a friend (Proverbs 27:17).

Friends who draw you closer to God are a tremendous gift. Mike and I are blessed to be close with several couples we can go to for prayer. These men and women are trustworthy and full of wisdom and encouragement.

Individually, my husband and I both have friends who provide us with godly counsel when needed. I'm thankful to have mighty women of faith in my life who lift me up in prayer. We laugh, shop, share stories, and pray together regularly. While my number one person to be with is always Mike, it is a blessing to have a fun laugh or a good cry with one of my best friends.

READ GOD'S WORD EVERY DAY

I've already mentioned this a few times (okay, more than a few times), but when you read God's Word, you find peace, wisdom, and strength. Do you want those things in your marriage? I know I do! Reading the Bible with your husband brings a special intimacy to your relationship. One way to do this is to read the same book of the Bible and then discuss what God shows to the two of you and says to your hearts.

As with praying, talking, and everything else, find a time that works best for your schedules. Young children often need attention during the day, so reading early in the morning or late in the evening may be preferable. The important thing is to make it happen.

SERVE EACH OTHER IN LOVE

Everyone has their own way of serving others. Mike has a wonderful servant's heart, and he shows his love for me by doing yardwork and helping around the house with laundry, cleaning, and cooking. He is an amazing cook! I am definitely a very blessed wife.

I, on the other hand, show my love to Mike through affirmation (words of appreciation and encouragement) and through the way I take care of our home—decorating, organizing, and making it a beautiful and comfortable place to rest and recharge. I also cook regularly. It's not my favorite thing to do, but it makes my husband happy, and that makes me happy. We both lovingly serve each other, just in different ways.

You and your husband may also have distinct serving styles. Choose to value each other's gifts and strengths, and don't withhold appreciation if something isn't done exactly to your liking. Serving one another in love will bless your relationship and build a strong marriage.

LOVE IS ...

Love is patient and kind. Love is not jealous or boastful or proud or rude. It does not demand its own way. It is not irritable, and it keeps no record of being wronged. It does not rejoice about injustice but rejoices whenever the truth wins out. Love never gives up, never loses faith, is always hopeful, and endures through every circumstance. Prophecy and speaking in unknown languages and special knowledge will become useless. But love will last forever! (1 Corinthians 13:4–8).

You and your husband are together on this journey called marriage. When you make your relationship a priority, the road of life is much more enjoyable to travel. Your love and devotion will show your children that the commitment you made to each other is important and second only to your commitment to the Lord.

> **When you make your relationship a priority, the road of life is much more enjoyable to travel.**

CHAPTER 7

STUDY GUIDE

REVIEW

The best foundation for parenting is a marriage that reflects the love of God. Make your relationship with your husband a priority and finds ways to communicate and connect on a daily basis. Commit to honor, forgive, value, and love each other. Above all, seek the Lord together and trust that He has a wonderful plan for your marriage.

SCRIPTURES

- Genesis 2:18–24
- Proverbs 31:10–31
- 1 Corinthians 13
- Ephesians 5:21–31

QUESTIONS

- In what areas of your marriage do you feel confident? In what areas would you like to grow?
- What are some thoughts, desires, or goals you would like to share with your husband?
- How can you speak words of life and encouragement over your relationship and still address conflict?

HEART CONNECTORS

- Write your husband a love letter and put it under his pillow. If you aren't married, write a letter to the Lord in your journal. Let Him know how much you love Him and how thankful you are for His love and faithfulness.

- Make a list of date ideas. Include simple, inexpensive things to do as well as more elaborate possibilities that you and your husband can plan for the future. Go over the list with your husband and mark dates on your calendar. If you happen to find yourselves with unexpected free time one day, seize the moment and have fun together!

PRAYER

Father God, thank You for my husband. He is a wonderful gift, and I am so grateful You brought us together. Please guide and direct us as we seek to grow in our relationship with each other and with You. I choose today to honor my husband through my thoughts, words, and actions. Help me be his number one encourager, helper, and partner. May our marriage be a representation of Your love for us. In Jesus' name, Amen.

CHAPTER 8

EVERY WORD COUNTS

The tongue can bring death or life;
those who love to talk will reap the consequences.

—Proverbs 18:21

W hat would you do if you knew your words could impact the future of your children? What would you say? As moms, we have an incredible, God-given opportunity not only to speak into our children's lives but also to have tremendous influence with those words. Our words are like seeds that are planted deep in our children's hearts and grow throughout their lives. Every mom needs to ask herself, *Am I regularly blessing my family? Or am I constantly focusing on their weaknesses and reminding them where they fall short?*

I am not suggesting we ignore bad behavior or turn a blind eye to issues that need to be corrected. If our children have areas in which they need guidance and discipline, then we should help them. However, there is a big difference between highlighting problem areas without offering help or hope and acknowledging that change is needed and focusing on working together. We can address situations with godly parental authority and speak life over our children at the same time.

> We can address situations with godly
> parental authority and speak life
> over our children at the same time.

LOOSE WORDS

When I became a Christian, one of the first things God did was clean up my mouth. The problem had started in high school when I would jokingly use inappropriate language. By the time I finished college, these words were part of my regular vocabulary. Then I submitted my life to the Lord, and He showed me that what I say matters. He opened my eyes to the effects of not only "bad" words but also negative language about myself and others. Since then, there have been times when I said things I later regretted, but I am much more careful about what I let come out of my mouth.

My sons used to tease me about my response to any kind of negative talk. I was known to rebuke loose words on a regular basis. Loose words are any words that do not bring life, edification, encouragement, or affirmation. Some examples of loose words and phrases are

- Stupid ("I'm not smart enough.")
- Slow ("I'm not fast enough.")
- Failure ("I'm not good enough.")
- Weak ("I'm not strong enough.")

I didn't allow loose words to be thrown about haphazardly in our home, our car, or anywhere else. Why? Because I knew if our family spoke negative words over ourselves, then we would begin to believe those words in our hearts. The enemy wants us to believe we have no value, but we must remember that he is a liar (see John 8:44). Our heavenly Father made us and loves us. We have value because we belong to Him!

I was quick to address negative words spoken by my sons, and I was also quick to rebuke loose words spoken over them by others. These rebukes were usually silent because I realized most people had no ill intent. You have probably heard some of these "innocent" remarks:

- "That child can't sit still!"
- "Boys will be boys." ("Girls will be girls.")
- "They may listen to you now but wait till they get older."

The last one was my least favorite, and sometimes I couldn't help but answer back (in a kind way, of course). I would gently say, "My sons are obedient now and will continue to be obedient as they get older." I wasn't trying to shame the other person, but I knew it was important to speak words of life over my children.

Will we as moms get this aspect of parenting right every time? I wish it were possible to give an honest "yes," but the truth is we're not always going to say the right thing at the right time. Sometimes our words won't be as edifying as we would like them to be, and we will wish we could take them back. In these moments of weakness, we can set a godly example by apologizing to our children. Telling them we are sorry for not being kind with our words and asking for their forgiveness lets them know that apologizing is the right thing to do. It tells them that all of us (even parents) make mistakes. All of us need a Savior.

ENCOURAGEMENT: WHY AND HOW?

Beginning when our sons were young, Mike and I made it a point to encourage them and speak God's Word over them as often as possible. We knew our words would have a lifetime impact, and we wanted that impact to be positive and full of blessing. Encouraging words ministered to our sons' hearts much more than discouraging remarks for errors they made.

When correction was needed, we lovingly helped the boys learn from their mistakes so they could move forward and do better in the future. In a world that doesn't always offer life-giving words, we realized that we were the most important source of encouragement for our sons.

Every child is unique. You may have to do some detective work to find out what kind of encouragement works best for each one. As I've mentioned before, our sons loved playing tennis, and our family spent many days, nights, and weekends on the tennis courts. I was not a cheerleader in high school, but you would have never known that if you saw, or rather *heard*, me at tennis tournaments. I cheered the boys on with gusto! When I learned that Joel was not a fan of having his name yelled out, I resorted to lots of clapping and silently raising a triumphant fist in the air. Jacob, however, liked a louder kind of cheering. He let me know at a tournament one day that he couldn't hear my voice, and from then on, I made sure he could always hear me cheering for him. Both sons wanted encouragement—they just desired it in different ways. If you're not sure of the best way to encourage your children, then ask them. They will tell you!

Another thing I did to encourage my sons was to let them hear me sharing good things about them with friends and extended family. Have you ever overheard someone you love talking about you in glowing terms? Doesn't it feel good to know you are highly thought of and cared about? Children need affirmation and validation too. Remember, encouragement is not about bragging or being prideful. Instead, it's about recognizing your children's strengths and celebrating their efforts.

GIFTS AND CALLINGS

What gifting do you see in your children? In Chapter 5, I talked about how some strengths are easy to spot while others may take more time to uncover. It is possible that some of the things you see right now are not what you would normally consider "gifts." For example, your little boy may like to sing all day long at the top of his lungs. Getting the baby to sleep through all the singing might be a challenge, but could your son be a future worship leader, singer, or songwriter? Maybe your little girl always has something to say about everything. She might be a future teacher, writer, or public speaker. Then there's the child who constantly paints or draws, and not only on paper—his designs are also on your home's walls and floors. He could be your up-and-coming artist, illustrator, or architect. Granted, these children may just like to sing out loud, talk all the time, and color on whatever is available, but don't discount the possibility of something that could be a life calling.

> Don't discount the possibility of something that could be a life calling.

Speak life over your children as they try new things and discover their passions. For some children, the discovery process is simple and quick. They know right away what they like, and they are eager to grow in their strengths and overcome their weaknesses. Other children take a bit longer. They want to explore all their options and even try a few out before committing to one thing. Either way, you have the privilege of a front row seat to watch, encourage, and pray.

Seek God's heart for each of your children. He knows what their strengths and giftings are because He gave those things to your little ones. When you ask the Lord to give you a word of encouragement for one of your children, He will! He may show you a Scripture that rings true about your child or give you an encouraging thought about him or her while you are praying. Write down whatever the Lord says to you and share it with your child.

One day when my older son, Jacob, was around 10 years old, we were both sitting and reading in our family room. I looked up and saw him, and the Lord immediately spoke to my heart about him. I said, "Jacob, you are going to be a great father. The Lord wants you to know this." I went on to encourage him in this area. Over the years, the Lord has given Mike and me words of encouragement for both our sons. As I was writing these words, Joel walked into my room, and I reminded him that from the time he was a young boy, it has been spoken over him that he is a warrior. For many years, Joel planned to join the military. As he got older, though, Mike and I sensed that he was a warrior in the spiritual realm—one whose prayers would bring freedom to others. We never told him our thoughts on this matter, because we knew God would speak to our son's heart if this was indeed His plan. As a young adult, Joel told us that he believed God had shown him a different plan for his life and that he would not be joining the military after all. Joel is still a warrior today, and the battles he fights are for the kingdom of God.

LOUD AND LOVING SILENCE

Many parents feel compelled to say something every time their children misbehave or have mishaps. Sometimes, though, it's what we don't say that speaks volumes. There will be moments when your children know they have done something wrong before you even mention it. Misbehavior is not always accompanied by the intent to be disobedient or rebellious. Children can become so caught up in having fun that they make a mess of their rooms or accidentally break a piece of décor. Maybe they feel rather artistic one afternoon and enthusiastically draw and write on the hardwood floors with black markers. (This marker incident may or may not have happened at our house.) When they realize what they have done, a hug from you can say what words cannot.

Proverbs 25:11 says,

> Timely advice is lovely,
>   like golden apples in a silver basket.

Timing really is everything, isn't it? It is so important to pray about how and when to speak into a situation, especially with older and adult children. Only you can know if you have enough relational equity to share what's on your heart. When in doubt, take the issue to the Lord. He will direct you, and if you are supposed to say something, He will give you the right words. As a mom of adult, married sons, I make a conscious effort not to offer advice, counsel, or opinions unless asked. If I do have something I'd like to share, then I try to preface it with, "May I speak into that?" or "I'm submitting this to you to think about." I don't always get it right, but the desire of my heart is to respect my sons, their wives, and their decisions. Respect doesn't mean we have to agree on everything. Instead, it means we trust each other and honor each other's decisions.

///////

God is the Creator and Sustainer of life, and at the beginning of time, He spoke everything into existence (see Genesis 1). We humans are certainly not as powerful as God is, but our words still carry great authority. What are your words speaking into existence in your family? Are you speaking life or death over your children? Every word counts. Your words are a bridge to your children's hearts, and life-giving communication will keep those hearts open to a relationship with you and with God.

> Your words are a bridge
> to your children's hearts.

CHAPTER 8

STUDY GUIDE

REVIEW

Words have tremendous influence on the lives of our children. We must carefully guard against any negative language that would give the enemy access to their hearts. As parents, we are the most important source of encouragement for our children, and even when correction is needed, we can still speak life as we help them learn from their mistakes. The Lord has a special purpose for each of our children, and it is our privilege to cheer them on as we watch and pray.

SCRIPTURES

- Psalm 19
- Psalm 34:12–14
- Proverbs 16:23–24
- James 3:2–12

QUESTIONS

- What are some loose words you need to rebuke in your family and even in your own heart?
- How can you speak life over your children as you correct them?
- In what ways does each of your children like to be encouraged?

HEART CONNECTORS

- Make a 31-day calendar with a Scripture and a life-giving word or phrase for each day. Put it in a place where everyone in the family can see it (refrigerator door, bathroom mirror, etc.), or if your children are older, send it to them through text or email. This calendar is something your children can read every day to keep God's Word in their hearts, and it's also a daily reminder of your love for them.

- Make it a habit to pray God's Word over your children. Ask the Lord to show you specific Scriptures and words of encouragement for each child. Write these Scriptures and words in a journal and give it to your child. This priceless gift can be given anytime, and it makes a wonderful present for special milestone occasions (birthday, graduation, wedding, etc.).

PRAYER

Father God, thank You that every word from You is loving, kind, and full of life. Please help me remember that the things I say have a lasting impact on my children. Show me how to speak life over them in every situation and let me be quick to repent when I say things I should not. I pray my children will feel loved, supported, and encouraged as they discover Your amazing plan for their lives. Thank You for the privilege of being their mom. In Jesus' name, Amen.

CHAPTER 9

DUST KICKERS

He got up from the meal, took off his outer clothing, and wrapped a towel around his waist. After that, he poured water into a basin and began to wash his disciples' feet, drying them with the towel that was wrapped around him.

— John 13:4–5 (NIV)

You might wonder why a chapter titled "Dust Kickers" would begin with a verse about Jesus washing His disciples' feet. I will explain in a moment, but first let's look at a Scripture in two different Bible translations.

This letter is from Paul and Timothy, slaves of Christ Jesus.
I am writing to all of God's holy people in Philippi who belong to Christ Jesus, including the church leaders and **deacons** (Philippians 1:1 NLT, bold added).

Dear friends in Philippi,
My name is Paul and I'm joined by Timothy, both of us servants of Jesus, the Anointed One. We write this letter to all his devoted followers in your city, including your pastors, and to all the **servant-leaders** of the church (Philippians 1:1 TPT, bold added).

Which translation is correct? They both are. They say the same thing, just in two different ways. By reading a verse in more than one translation, we often get a clearer picture and a greater understanding of what it means. The word *deacons* in the New Living Translation is rendered *servant-leaders* in The Passion Translation. A footnote in the latter translation states the following:

> As translated from the Aramaic. The Greek text is "deacons." The word for deacon is actually taken from a Greek compound of the words *dia* and *kovis* that means "to kick up the dust," referring to a servant who is so swift to accomplish his service that he stirs up the dust of the street running to fulfill his duty.[6]

The first time I read this footnote, I thought to myself, *That sounds like a mom!* When our children need us, we are quick to respond. Yes, it may take us a moment or two to gather our bearings in the middle of the night, but once we are awake, we feed our hungry babies and change their dirty diapers. We bandage our toddlers' scraped knees, help our older children with their homework, and support our adult children in their endeavors. Quick with prayer, fast with encouragement, and swift with affection, we are dust kickers!

OUR SERVANT-HEARTED SAVIOR

What does dust kicking have to do with Jesus washing His disciples' feet? It's all about the attitude of the heart. In John 13 we read about the last meal Jesus shared with His twelve closest companions before His arrest and crucifixion. Here are verses 4–5 again:

---

6. Brian Simmons, *The Passion Translation: New Testament with Psalms, Proverbs, and Song of Songs* (Savage, MN: BroadStreet Publishing, 2017), accessed July 29, 2020, https://classic.biblegateway.com/passage/?-search=philippians+1%3A1&version=TPT.

He got up from the meal, took off his outer clothing, and wrapped a towel around his waist. After that, he poured water into a basin and began to wash his disciples' feet, drying them with the towel that was wrapped around him (NIV).

Foot washing was the lowest form of servitude during that time. When people entered a home, their feet were dusty and dirty, and it was the job of a servant to wash them. The Son of God took the lowly position of a servant and washed dirty feet with the same hands that would soon be nailed to a cross.

Why did Jesus, whom Revelation 19:16 refers to "King of all kings and Lord of all lords," humble Himself in such a profound way? I believe the answer can be found in Matthew 20:

You know that the rulers in this world lord it over their people, and officials flaunt their authority over those under them. But among you it will be different. Whoever wants to be a leader among you must be your servant, and whoever wants to be first among you must become your slave. For even the Son of Man came not to be served but to serve others and to give his life as a ransom for many (vv. 25–28).

Throughout His ministry on earth, Jesus repeatedly demonstrated that a God-centered life is about serving others—family, friends, neighbors, and even strangers.

> **A God-centered life is about serving others.**

For years I wondered why Jesus removed His outer clothing (His robe) before washing the disciples' feet. Did He simply not want to get it wet and dirty, or was there more to it than that?

One day while studying the Bible, I learned that robes represented social status in Jewish society.[7] The act of removing His robe was a physical demonstration that Jesus, the Son of God and soon-to-be Savior of all humanity, laid aside His authority and chose to be a servant. The washing of the disciples' feet was a precursor to Jesus laying down His life on the cross.

As believers, we demonstrate Jesus' love by laying aside our wants and desires in order to serve others. This is especially true for moms. We make many sacrifices as we care for our families, and in doing so we give our children a godly example of servant-hearted leadership. I believe that when we do this, we are most in alignment with Christ's heart for us.

When my son Joel was a little boy, he loved being outside and playing in the dirt. I regularly had to remind him to wipe his feet before coming inside the house. One day Joel was playing outside, and the ground was wet from recent rain. I heard the door open, and I turned around to find him standing just inside the house with both bare feet covered in mud. I thought I was going to be upset, but his cute three-year-old face just looked at me, seemingly wondering, *What is Mom going to do?* Without saying a word, I picked him up, carried him to the bathroom, and sat him on the counter. I turned on the water faucet, and we waited silently for the water to warm up. Then I filled the sink and put his muddy little feet in the warm water, gently washing them off with soap. When I was done, I dried his feet, hugged him, and gave him lots of kisses. Joel gave me the biggest smile. Then I said he could go back outside to play.

That memory stands out in my mind as a reminder of how we're called to serve those we love. Life gets messy, and instead of getting upset about it, we can choose to show love and

7. Martin H. Manser, "DICTIONARY OF BIBLE THEMES—5177 ROBES," BibleGateway.com, 2009, https://classic.biblegateway.com/resources/dictionary-of-bible-themes/5177-robes.

patience. When I brought up this story with Joel recently, I was surprised to learn that he didn't remember it at all. I was a little sad at first, because it was such a sweet moment. However, I've come to realize that this story is for me. You see, foot washing is part of being a mom, both figuratively and literally. Our children will not always remember everything we said or did, but they are likely to remember being showered with love when they expected something entirely different.

AN ORGANIZED HOME

Two of my favorite dust-kicking hobbies are organizing and reading about organizing. It's so much fun to see what can be done to bring more order and beauty to my home. Does that mean I am the champion of organization? Not at all. I still have a few overstuffed closets and drawers. Sometimes my pantry doesn't have the things I need because I forget to go to the grocery store, and I don't dust or vacuum as often as I probably should. But I still like reading about all the things I could do and all the things I don't do!

From the time my sons were young until they got married and moved out, they were a big part of keeping our home in order. They helped clean, and as they got older, they did their own laundry. I wanted them to be ready to help their future wives one day. When we encourage our children to help us around the house, we are telling them that our family is a team, and as a team, we all take care of our home. I remember one day of housecleaning in particular when the boys were young. Joel asked, "Who's coming over?" He thought that because we were making the house look nice, we must be having company over that evening. That moment served as a teaching time for both of us. I told Joel we weren't having guests that day; instead, we were cleaning up for ourselves so that our home would be nice and comfortable for our family. I then told myself that I needed to be aware of the message I was sending that seemed to imply we only cleaned when company is coming.

> When we encourage our children to help us around the house, we are telling them that our family is a team, and as a team, we all take care of our home.

I once spoke with a mom who felt guilty about asking her children to help around the house. My encouragement to her was that we do a disservice to our children when we don't teach and allow them to help take care of our home. It's important that every member of the family works together to help make the home a beautiful and comfortable place to live. We teach our children to be helpful when we include them in our cleaning efforts. Additionally, we prepare them to be able to keep their future homes in order and be blessings to their future spouses.

There are many different methods of organization, and only you can determine what works best for your family. Here are two ideas that have helped me keep my home (and my life) better organized over the years:

MAKE LISTS

I love lists. They help me take everything that's swirling around in my brain and put it on paper where I can see it and manage it. Another benefit of lists is that they show your children and your spouse specific ways to help you. Young children may see cleaning as a fun game. Let them help you, even if it means some follow-up cleaning on your part. Even toddlers can tidy up by putting their toys away in a big basket. They may not do everything perfectly, but they are learning, and their excitement to help with chores is a good thing.

If making lists is new to you, I recommend beginning by making a master list of every task you need to do, want to do, and would do if you had time or lived in an alternate universe. Next, make three individual lists: daily, weekly, and monthly. Assign each task to one of the individual lists.

Your daily list might include making the beds, wiping down the bathroom and kitchen counters, doing a load or two of laundry and putting the clean clothes away, and sweeping the kitchen. Include anything you would like to get done on a daily basis. It's okay if your list looks different than mine or anyone else's—we all have different things we like to get done each day.

You weekly list might include cleaning out the refrigerator, deep cleaning the bathroom, vacuuming rugs and carpets, dusting furniture, washing bedding, planning the next week's menu, and grocery shopping. It's helpful to have a menu prepared for the upcoming week and to shop for the necessary ingredients ahead of time. When first starting this schedule, do your grocery shopping for the next two weeks to give yourself a head start. Also, when forming your weekly list, assign one or two items to certain days of the week. For example, you might write, "Vacuum and dust on Tuesdays." Leave one day open for any catching up you may need to do.

Your monthly list might include dusting ceiling fans, wiping down baseboards, and any home maintenance repairs that need to be done. These tasks generally need doing only every four or five weeks. To prevent clutter from taking over, you can also choose one room each month (or every other month) to clean out. Remove the things that are no longer useful to you or your family, such as old toys, games, clothes, or décor, and decide what to donate and what to throw away.

Now here is my disclaimer to lists: I don't always follow them. Surprising, I know, because I really do enjoy making and having

THE JOY OF BEING MOM

lists. There are times when I simply can't get everything done. The great thing about lists, though, is that they are tools to help you, not to make you feel bad if you miss a day or a week. Use them when you can, and when you can't, give yourself a break and try again the next day.

SCHEDULE FREE EVENINGS

A clean, comfortable home is important, but so is rest and relaxation. If every evening is filled with something to do or somewhere to go, then you and your family can easily become tired and worn out. Schedule free evenings with no tasks or engagements on the same days each week. Yes, there will be times when you have to attend to something important on a free night, but those occasions should be the exception and not the norm.

IT'S ALL WORTH IT!

Many of our life choices as moms are dictated by the needs of our families. Do we sacrifice? Yes. Do we get tired? Yes. Do we sometimes feel depleted? Yes. Is it all worth it? A resounding yes! Let me encourage you with this thought: everything you do as a mother ministers to your family. By putting your family's needs and desires ahead of your own, you demonstrate the sacrificial love of Jesus Christ.

Motherhood is all about serving. There are seasons when we may need to lay aside our "robe" as Jesus did in order to be available for our children. Some moms work outside the home full-time while others work at home full-time. Some do full-time volunteer work, and others do a little of this and a little of that. The bottom line is that *all* mothers work full-time in one way or another. Laying aside your desires for the sake of your family can be difficult, especially when you are not sure how long the season will last. I can assure you, though, that God is faithful. If He puts a dream in your heart, then He will make it come to pass in His perfect timing. The key to contentment in whatever your circumstances may be is your relationship with the Lord and your trust in His plan for your life.

Ladies, let's support, pray for, and encourage each other in hearing God speak to us about our lives. It's easy to pick a side regarding whether moms should stay home or whether they should work full-time or do a bit of both. The truth is every decision a mom makes is between her and the Lord. When we surrender our lives to Him, we can trust that when we prayerfully ask Him for direction, He will guide us. Every woman (along with her husband if she's married) must seek God's heart for what He wants her mom-life to look like.

When Mike and I lived in Orlando as newlyweds, I had a friend who was a new mom. I would call and ask her how she was doing, and her reply was always the same: "I'm dying to myself." I didn't understand what she meant until I became a mom. As I cared for my family, their needs became more important than my own. Some people warned me that being so engrossed in the lives of my husband and sons could cause me to "lose my identity." That didn't happen, though. Instead, I found my identity—not in my family, but in the Lord. I learned that by serving my family, I am serving the Lord, and that brings me great joy. Dying to myself really does bring life!

KICKING UP SOME DUST

There are so many ways moms serve their children. From the time our little ones wake up to the time they go to bed, our days are filled with diapers, feeding, cleaning, laundry, and a myriad of other essential tasks. If you work outside of the home, then your "home" work begins the moment you walk in the door. Older children can do more and more things for themselves, but we still have plenty of mom duties. I'm not trying to sound discouraging—I'm just saying that moms have a lot to do. We get tired sometimes, and we don't always feel seen or appreciated.

Here's a truth that I pray brings comfort to your heart and mind: God sees you, and He appreciates everything you're doing for His children. He sees all your daily sacrifices. He understands that when you serve, you put others' needs above your own. Your Christ-like nature is on full display, and God is so proud of you. You set a wonderful example for your children to follow, and with the Lord's help, they will become servant-hearted dust kickers too!

> God sees you, and He appreciates everything you're doing for His children.

CHAPTER 9

STUDY GUIDE

REVIEW

Moms are servant-leaders. We make sacrifices and lay aside our wants and desires in order to serve our families. When our children help around the house, they learn that every member of the family plays an important role in making the home comfortable and beautiful. As moms, we can find contentment in any circumstance by remembering that God sees us, loves us, and will make our dreams come to pass in His perfect timing.

SCRIPTURES

- Psalm 86:1–7
- Proverbs 31:10–31
- Romans 12:10–12
- Titus 2:3–5

QUESTIONS

- Why did Jesus remove His robe before washing His disciples' feet?
- What are two or three goals you would like to achieve regarding your home?
- How can you encourage yourself when you feel unseen and unappreciated?

HEART CONNECTORS

- Make a list of everything that needs to be done in your house, dividing the tasks into daily, weekly, and monthly lists. Then share these lists with your family. Explain that a clean and comfortable home requires teamwork and invite each of your children to take ownership of a task. When you see your children either completing or making an effort to complete their tasks, let them know that you are proud of their servant hearts and that God is too.

- In your quiet time, talk to God about your dreams and desires. Ask Him to help you wait patiently during seasons of serving your family. If you are feeling discouraged or defeated in your role as a mom, be honest with God. Ask Him to speak to your heart and give you His peace and joy. God may show you an encouraging Scripture or speak to you through a comforting friend. Record these things in your journal and thank God for His faithfulness.

PRAYER

Father God, thank You for giving Your Son, Jesus, to be the ultimate example of servant leadership. I want to show Your love to my family through my words and actions. Please help me remember that even if no one else sees the sacrifices I make, You see them. I trust Your plan for my life, and I submit all my dreams and desires to Your perfect timing. I pray that my children will be blessed by my example and develop servant hearts of their own. In Jesus' name, Amen.

CHAPTER 10

WHAT'S YOUR VISION?

When people do not accept divine guidance, they run wild.
—Proverbs 29:18

You'll never get to your destination if you don't know where you're going. Without divine guidance or vision, we go this way and that way and end up nowhere. It's easy to get frustrated with ourselves and with life in general when it feels as if we aren't making progress or achieving satisfactory results. I used to tell myself after long days, "Tomorrow will be different." I really meant it when I said it, but without any kind of plan, schedule, or even a simple to-do list, I found myself making the same empty promise day after day. Can you relate? If so, then this chapter is for you.

IT IS WHAT IT IS ... OR IS IT?

I have a love-hate relationship with the phrase, "It is what it is." I love the idea that whether I like a situation or not, I can be realistic about it. However, I've come to realize that for some scenarios, a more accurate phrase is, "It isn't what I think it is."

Over the years I've noticed that people make plans about lots of things. We plan where we want to live, what kind of house we want to have, and how we want to decorate the interior and exterior of our home. When we buy a car, we spend time researching different makes and models, choosing must-have features, and comparing prices before committing to the big buy. However, when it comes to parenthood, there isn't always a lot of planning involved. Yes, we may plan the nursery, searching magazines and websites to find the colors, furniture, and décor that will make the room look just right. It's fun to dream and decorate. Putting together a beautiful nursery for your baby is a way to celebrate his or her upcoming arrival. It's good memory making, and I'm all about making good family memories.

So what is the problem? you may wonder. The problem is that we sometimes spend more time planning our dream house, researching our dream car, or designing our dream nursery than we do praying about being a parent. Sometimes it's easier to just "wing it." After all, how hard can it be? Haven't people been having children forever? In one sense, that is true—babies are born every day. These beautiful, tiny humans just want to be loved, fed, and taken care of by their parents. "Taken care of" has a rather broad definition, though. One of the most important things Mike and I learned early on was the significance of having a vision for our parenting. There were many questions to be answered:

- What kind of parents did we want to be?
- How could we parent our children in a way that would draw them close to us and the Lord?
- What kind of relationship did we want to have with our children?
- What kind of relationship did we want our children to have with each other?

We needed a plan. We needed a strategy. We needed a vision.

Anything we wish to do well in life requires planning, time, patience, work, and prayer. Motherhood is no different. Vision is important because it helps determine the decisions we make on a regular basis. If I have a vision to lose weight, then I can't eat ice cream every day. (I know it's easier said than done—I love ice cream too.) Proverbs 29:18 says, "Where there is no vision, the people perish" (KJV). How do we get a vision for life, marriage, and parenting? We seek God's heart by reading His Word and praying for His wisdom and guidance. When we have vision from God, we can focus more clearly on Him and what He desires for us and our families.

> Anything we wish to do well in life requires planning, time, patience, work, and prayer. Motherhood is no different.

Here are some things to consider when seeking God's vision:

- For Yourself
  - Relationship with the Lord
  - Being a wife
  - Being a mom
  - Relationships with extended family and friends
  - Educational goals
  - Work/Business goals
  - Godly counsel, if needed
- For Your Marriage
  - Praying together
  - Church involvement
  - Serving each other
  - Scheduling dates, vacations, vision retreats, and vision talks (as a couple and as family)
  - Marriage retreats and conferences
  - Godly counsel, if needed
  - Fellowship

- For Your Children
  - Relationships with the Lord
  - Relationships with siblings
  - Education
  - Relationships with friends

I encourage you to use these lists as a starting point and add any additional topics or categories as you see fit. You may already have some great vision ideas for yourself as a mom and wife and some equally amazing ideas for your children. Just remember that the best vision ideas come straight from God's heart. When we have His plan in focus, we position ourselves to receive the wonderful things He has in store for us and our families.

SIMPLE STEPS FOR VISION PLANNING

PRAY, LISTEN, AND READ

> Be still in the presence of the LORD,
>   and wait patiently for him to act (Psalm 37:7).

Praying and listening work best when done in that order. When we have preconceived ideas for ourselves or our families, it's easy to go with what we think before truly taking it to God. We need to pray first and then listen for His voice. After praying, we may feel reassured of our initial thoughts, but it's always best to pray first with an open mind and heart.

Reading the Bible on a daily basis is also important because doing so helps us learn to recognize God's voice and what He wants to tell us. You see, the enemy wants to speak to us as well, and his voice is the one that says we are useless, worthless, and unable to be good moms because of our past mistakes. Satan would have us believe that God doesn't love us and that we are not really saved. If he has been saying any of those lies to you, then let me encourage you. When you acknowledged your need for a Savior, repented of your sins, and asked Jesus to take control of your life, He did! You are safe in the arms of your heavenly Father. God does not speak to His children with words of condemnation, anger, shame, or abandonment. In John 10:27–29, Jesus says,

> My sheep listen to my voice; I know them, and they follow me. I give them eternal life, and they will never perish. No one can snatch them away from me, for my Father has given them to me, and he is more powerful than anyone else. No one can snatch them from the Father's hand.

God does not speak to His children with words of condemnation, anger, shame, or abandonment.

Having Scripture planted in our hearts allows us to know who we are in God and also who He is and how much He loves us. Most people don't hear God's audible voice with their ears, but we know it's Him in our hearts and minds. His leading and guidance will never contradict His Word.

When we read the Word and talk to God in prayer, we posture our hearts to hear what He wants to tell us. Psalm 5:3 says,

> Listen to my voice in the morning, LORD.
> Each morning I bring my requests to you and wait expectantly.

The Passion Translation says it this way:

> At each and every sunrise you will hear my voice
> as I prepare my *sacrifice of* prayer to you.

Every morning I lay out the pieces of my life on the altar
and wait *for your fire to fall upon my heart.*

A common concern is, *How can I know for sure that I'm hearing God and not just listening to my own thoughts?* Because we are human, it is possible to get the two confused sometimes. However, the more time we spend in the Word, the more we will be able to know and recognize God's voice.

WRITE EVERYTHING DOWN

As you read God's Word and pray, write down your hopes and dreams for the future. Make a list of desires for yourself, your marriage, your children, and anything else that is on your heart. You may wonder, *Doesn't God already know what's on my heart?* Yes, He does. Writing these things down is for your benefit, not His. It will help you organize your thoughts about yourself and your family and highlight what is important to you in this particular season of life. You will also want to write down what the Lord impresses upon your heart.

The following Scripture has been my life verse for many years:

Take delight in the LORD,
and he will give you your heart's desires (Psalm 37:4).

At first, it sounds like all I have to do is to be excited about God and He will give me everything I want. But there's a bit more to it than that. The first part of the verse says, "Take delight in the LORD." Focus on Him. Praise Him for His loving, kind, and faithful nature. Celebrate His healing, restoration, peace, joy, and so much more. When we put God first in our lives, our hearts come into alignment with His heart. We begin to want for ourselves what He wants for us. His desires become our desires, and because we are now in sync with His will, we see our prayers answered. Amazing, isn't it?

CLARIFY YOUR VISION

After writing down everything God has shown you in His Word and spoken to your heart, go back and *patiently* read what you have written. Why do I emphasize patience? Because this step can take time, and you don't want to become annoyed or worried about getting it done. I encourage you to enjoy the process of clarifying your vision. Add any new ideas to the list and delete existing ones that don't quite fit. If there is something you are unsure about, then continue praying and asking the Lord for wisdom. You can also seek godly counsel from trusted family, friends, or church leaders.

FORMULATE YOUR PLAN

You are now ready to formulate your plan. You may realize that some parts of your vision are for today, while other parts are for a later date and time. Put your "future vision" plans in a place where you won't forget where they are waiting. In God's timing you'll pull them out, maybe make some revisions, and get started. For now, it's time to focus on what God has put on your heart for today.

As always, continue to seek the Lord as you put your plan together. This is not a business contract that must be followed word for word; instead, it is a reminder of the vision God has shown you for yourself, your marriage, and your children. Let the plan be a written declaration and prayer of what you hope to accomplish in the next season. As you move forward, your situation may change, and there may be parts of the original vision that no longer fit. Be flexible and trust God to give you wisdom.

Display a written copy of your vision in a place where the entire family can easily see it. The purpose of this reminder is to help you, your husband, and your children succeed in the areas in which you want to accomplish certain goals. However, the vision should never take the place of praying and hearing the Lord every day. Review your list of dreams and desires every few months. Keep track of your progress, continue to pray, and allow God to be in control of your direction.

READY. SET. RELEASE!

Children are a gift from the LORD;
    they are a reward from him.
Children born to a young man
    are like arrows in a warrior's hands.
How joyful is the man whose quiver is full of them!
(Psalm 127:3–5).

I find it fascinating that this Scripture compares our children to arrows. Arrows are made to be sent out with a purpose, and the same is true of our children. Every child has a purpose, and in God's perfect timing, he or she will begin walking in that special calling. Are you putting into practice now what will enable and empower your children to hit the mark in the future?

When an arrow is released into the air, there are multiple factors that influence whether it will reach the desired target or not. These factors include wind, temperature, sunlight, tension of the bow, and, of course, the archer. As parents, we are the archers who hold our children's hearts and prepare them to be released. The countless decisions we make during the course of their childhood and young adult years will affect the direction of their lives. This is not meant to bring you fear or worry but to help bolster your praying and planning. As you help your children learn to hear God and trust His leading, you will all see that God "causes everything to work together" for good (Romans 8:28).

> The countless decisions we make during the course of their childhood and young adult years will affect the direction of their lives.

Vision provides direction. Ask yourself, *Where am I aiming my children?* If there is no target, then what are they going to hit? One of the benefits of having God's vision for your children is that He will direct your steps. A vision also sets a boundary that helps you make daily, ongoing decisions for yourself and your family.

My husband and I have a small ranch that is about 90 minutes away from our home in town. We go to this country property to relax, enjoy nature, and spend uninterrupted family time together. At the entrance, there's a gate with a lock. You must have a key to get inside. Now, if a thief really wanted to, he could drive straight through the gate, but he would probably hurt himself and his vehicle. Or he could climb over the gate (it's not very tall), but he would likely have problems getting to our house and carrying away the things he wants to steal. My point is that while someone potentially could break in and cause problems, it would be difficult because we have done everything we can to keep our ranch safe from harm.

By the way, humans are not the only threat out in the country. Wild animals such as coyotes and feral pigs can wreak havoc too. Some ranchers and farmers put up high fences to keep these pests out. You see, when you know there is the possibility of danger, you do all you can to protect the people you love. Boundaries provide protection. They help Mike and me protect our ranch, and they will help you make decisions that protect the things and people you love.

If you are married, then your greatest treasure is your spouse, followed by your children. Just as having a vision for your marriage will help guide your relationship, having a vision for parenting your children will help you determine what is and is not important for their future. Here are a few questions to ask yourself:

- What is the most important thing I want my children to know?
- What can I do to help them?
- What do I want our relationship to look like when they are adults?
- What do I hope their relationship with God looks like in the future?

Make decisions with the end goal in mind. Remember, the Lord has a specific plan for every family, and each of your children is a part of His plan.

> We can make our plans,
> but the LORD determines our steps (Proverbs 16:9).

WHAT ABOUT ADULT CHILDREN?

I realize some moms with adult children may be reading this and wondering, *What can I do now that my children are grown?* As I mentioned in a previous chapter, it's never too late to "build on the relationship you have with your adult children," even if they are already out of the house. However, if your relationship is strained, it may take time, patience, and prayer. If there has been hurt, disagreement, or a parting of ways, then prayerfully consider writing them a letter or card. Let them know you would like to continue writing to them and would welcome a response if or when they are ready.

If you choose to write, then do so with love. This is not the time for accusations, corrections, or demands for apologies or confessions. Instead, focus on how you can love your children through your words. Admit and apologize for your part in the situation. Although it may be difficult, try not to have any expectations regarding a reply. It may take time for your children to respond. Meanwhile, unless they ask you to stop writing, continue reaching out through cards and letters. Keep asking God to soften all your hearts and to make a way for reconciliation in His perfect timing.

CHAPTER 10

STUDY GUIDE

REVIEW

Every mom needs a vision for herself, her marriage, and her children. We often have our own hopes and dreams, but the best vision ideas come straight from God's heart. He will give us wisdom as we spend time praying and reading His Word. Vision helps determine the decisions we make on a regular basis. When we have God's plan in focus, we position ourselves to receive the wonderful things He has in store for us and our families.

SCRIPTURES

- Psalm 16:5–8
- Psalm 127
- Psalm 138
- Ephesians 1:15–18

QUESTIONS

- Why do you think some people spend less time praying about being parents than they do planning other aspects of their lives?
- What dreams or desires has God put on your heart for yourself, your marriage, or your children?
- Is the relationship you have with your children what you want it to be? If not, what can you start doing today to make things better?

HEART CONNECTORS

- Think about your vision for your children and ask the Lord, *What boundaries do I need to set to help protect them?* Write what He says to you in your journal. Refer to these boundaries when making decisions. As your children grow older, continue asking the Lord for His guidance. The boundaries may change over time, but His love for your family will always remain constant.

- Schedule a special time with your husband and children to talk about the vision for your family. Share the ideas God has put on your heart and invite your children to share any hopes and dreams they have as well. From this discussion, write a family vision statement. Display the statement prominently in your home and allow it to be a reminder of the direction God has for your family.

PRAYER

Father God, thank You for Your perfect vision for myself, my marriage, and my children. I am so grateful for Your wisdom and guidance. Please help me quiet my heart so I can hear Your voice. I want my dreams and desires to be in sync with Your will. Please strengthen, guide, and empower my children to walk in their calling and in Your ways all the days of their lives. In Jesus' name, Amen.

CHAPTER 11

A LASTING LEGACY

Keep putting into practice all you learned and received from me—everything you heard from me and saw me doing. Then the God of peace will be with you.

—Philippians 4:9

In Chapter 4, I talked about the joy of sharing family stories. But what if you feel as though your family stories aren't worth sharing? The truth is we don't all have sweet or pleasant memories to share. However, we can share what God has done to redeem our lives and our futures. We can share how He brought us from a place of pain to a place of healing and restoration. If this is your family's story, then it is part of your family's legacy too.

The dictionary has several entries for *legacy*, but in regard to family relations, the definition of this word is "something transmitted by or received from an ancestor or predecessor or from the past."[8] Legacy can refer to tangible items like money, but it also includes intangible things such as love, respect, and generosity. The latter are wonderful gifts that can be passed down from one generation to the next without ever decreasing. Here are some questions to think about regarding your family's legacy:

---

8. *Merriam-Webster.com Dictionary*, *s.v.* "legacy," accessed August 7, 2020, https://www.merriam-webster.com/dictionary/legacy.

- How do you want your family to be remembered?
- What do you want others to think of when they hear your family's name?
- Do you want your family to be known for
  - passionate praying?
  - generous hospitality?
  - extravagant giving?

Whether we plan to or not, we all have a legacy. This goes for everyone, regardless of marital status, parenting status, and any other status. What will your legacy be? A great place to start is the vision God has put on your heart. What stands out to you? What is at the core of who your family is to the world? Seek God's direction. You may have an idea right away because those who know and love you will already have seen the outward signs of what God has done and continues to do in your life.

MAKING A LEGACY

Your family may be known for many wonderful attributes, but the greatest legacy is an unwavering faith in Jesus Christ. A family that demonstrates its commitment to the Lord by loving and serving others on a daily basis is living out a godly legacy. A godly legacy is not about perfection, but rather about living a life that reflects the need for our Savior and brings Him honor and praise by sharing His heart and love for others.

> **The greatest legacy is an unwavering faith in Jesus Christ.**

Your family is a legacy in the making. Every moment is a possible memory to hold in your heart for generations to come. When you recognize the intangible gifts that were passed down to you, you realize the importance of stewarding what you have been given. Some of these gifts are lessons learned from the mistakes of past generations so that future loved ones can make wiser choices. Other gifts provide a strong foundation of past successes upon which to build and grow in the future. It is our responsibility to steward the blessings passed down to us and to continue adding to the legacy that has been established over generations.

At the time of writing this book, I am a Grammy (the grandmother name my sons gave me) to one sweet granddaughter in heaven. Poppy is Jacob and Neeli's baby girl who went to heaven because of a miscarriage. Although we never met Poppy we know we will see her one day in Heaven.

I am so blessed to see that our love of family and home continues on with our sons and daughters-in-love. Their homes are places of rest, peace, and the presence of God. Through God's grace, their children and their children's children will keep building upon this foundation and extend our legacy to future generations.

MY JOURNEY

I began writing this book with the intention of encouraging all the moms and moms-to-be out there. My hope was for you to find joy in every season of motherhood. I wanted to cheer you on and provide some helpful tips and ideas on parenting. Most of all, I wanted you to know that *you can do this*! God's Word tells us in Philippians 4:13, "I can do everything through Christ, who gives me strength."

However, something wonderfully unexpected happened during the writing process. As I began putting words to paper (or computer, rather), it became clear that this book was just as much for me as it is for other moms. Every story reminds me of God's love and faithfulness. Every victory belongs to Him, and every failure has been an opportunity to let Him hold my heart and help me try again. God transformed me from a woman who was nervous at the thought of having children to who I am today—a mom who passionately loves her family and truly delights in sharing the joys of motherhood.

Writing about my love for my children allowed me to recognize in a new way how much God loves me. It's not because of anything I do or don't do. He loves me just because I am His. And He loves you because you are His too! Let that sink in for a moment. God, the Creator of life and Sovereign Ruler of the universe, loves you because you are His.

When we recognize the never-ending and never-failing love of our heavenly Father, we are better able to face all that motherhood tries to throw at us. You know what I'm talking about—the feelings of exhaustion, fear, and inadequacy. The sleepless nights are more bearable when we know God gives us strength. The seasons of concern for children who may be making questionable decisions are less overwhelming when we know God gives us wisdom and direction. And in the moments when we feel depleted from sickness, loss, or confusion, we find great comfort in knowing that God sees us, holds us, and gives us everything we need. He loves us. He's our Father today and forever.

> When we recognize the never-ending and never-failing love of our heavenly Father, we are better able to face all that motherhood tries to throw at us.

My sons are adults now. They both have wives, jobs, and homes of their own. Parenting adult children is a whole new journey, and I am immensely grateful to be a welcome part of their lives. Mike and I are so proud of our sons, not because of our efforts as parents but because they have their own relationships with the Lord. Several years ago, Joel asked me how it felt when other people complimented him and his brother or complimented Mike and me regarding them. I told him that while it is nice to hear those words, I don't take credit for who he and Jacob are as young men. If I were to take the applause for all they accomplished, then I would also take the honor of their triumphs over difficult situations. Neither scenario would be fair.

Looking back at that conversation, I still feel the same way. As parents, Mike and I had the responsibility to lead our sons in the right direction and set a godly example, but it is their choices that ultimately determine their future. My prayer has always been that the foundation we set at home would give them the encouragement and vision to know they can do anything God calls them to do. I want them to know how deeply loved they are by their dad and me and that we will always be there for them. More than anything, my heart's desire is that they live their lives in full submission to the Lord.

Jacob and Joel have done well in allowing the Lord to work in their lives and help them grow in Him. They have shown maturity and wisdom in their adult years through both the good times and the challenging moments. It has been a joy to see them humbly walk in their victories and accomplishments. I now find myself learning from them quite regularly, and I like that a lot!

THE HOLY DAYS OF "I DO"

Aside from the days they were born, two of the most significant times in my life have been my sons' wedding days.

JACOB AND NEELI

Jacob was the first to get married. During the months of engagement, his fiancée (and now wife), Neeli, and her mom graciously included me in much of the wedding planning. This was such a sweet and wonderful surprise. Because my only daughter, Dani, is in heaven, I never thought I would have the joy of wedding planning for my children. I was overwhelmed and honored to be able to help and be a part of the preparations for the special day.

On the day of the wedding, I remember standing in the processional line and preparing to walk into the sanctuary with Jacob. I looked him in the eyes and said, "Son, I love you." I actually did that quite a few times as we got ready to walk in, but it was important to me for him to hear those words. Every "I love you" was my personal remembrance of that day and of what it symbolized. From the day Jacob and Neeli got engaged, they had taken steps toward beginning their life together. Mike and I would always be there for them, but this day was the culmination of years of preparation for our son to become the head of his family. I wanted him to know that I loved him, and I was proud of him.

JOEL AND DANNY

A few years later, it was Joel's turn. The parents of his fiancée (and now wife), Danny, live in Brazil, so I had the privilege and blessing of helping with all the wedding preparations. It was so much fun going to dress shops, buying shoes, visiting the florist, meeting with the venue coordinator, and doing all the other special activities.

One of my favorite memories is the day Danny chose her wedding dress. She walked out of the dressing room, and I couldn't help but smile. Danny later told me she knew it was *the dress* because when she walked out, I took a deep breath. She was right! I took lots of pictures of her in the dress, and the sales associate took pictures of the two of us. The most special part was when Danny called her mom in Brazil so she could see the dress. Within minutes, the mother and daughter were chatting away in Portuguese, and I took pictures of Danny wearing her dress and holding the phone with her mom's smiling face. I am so glad that Danny's mom got to have this special moment with her daughter. She even helped Danny pick out a veil over the phone. It was a beautiful day filled with beautiful memories.

On the morning of the wedding, I rode in the car with Joel to the wedding venue. We talked and laughed, and I just sat there enjoying the last bit of time with him before he became a husband. Truth be told, he doesn't remember much about our drive that morning, but that's okay, because I do. Later, as we stood at the back of the chapel waiting for our turn to walk in, I told him that I loved him and I was proud of the man he had grown to be. We were both so happy, and after I squeezed in "I love you" a few more times, we were ready to walk down the aisle.

LETTING GO

Your children may still be quite young, and perhaps the days of them getting married seem impossibly far away. However, from the moment children are born, we as parents begin the process of letting go.

- Babies rely on us completely for food, shelter, and love. We hold their tiny bodies and hearts close to keep them safe and secure.
- As they learn how to walk, we hold their little hands and help them stay steady. Then we let go and encourage them to keep going. Sometimes they fall, but they learn to get up and trust that our hands are just inches away to help them.
- When our children are young, we hold their hands to help them cross the street and move through crowded places. As they get older, they no longer need this physical guidance, but we keep our hands ready for encouraging pats on the back and much-needed hugs.
- In the adolescent years, our children begin learning to make decisions for themselves. There can be challenging moments, but they still need our attention, input, and love. Pats on the back and hugs can be more important than ever. Even though we may not have held their hands for a while, we still hold their hearts.

It can feel strange (and even sad) to realize our children need us less and less as they grow and mature, but it really is a good thing. Their dependence on us needs to decrease as their dependence on God increases. This does not mean we can't or won't be close to our children as they become adults. On the contrary, we can have wonderful relationships with them and be available whenever they need our input.

When our children are young, we have the upper hand in "discussions," but once they are older, things change. Adult children have their own thoughts, feelings, opinions, and ideas. And isn't that what we want? I think most parents hope their grown sons and daughters will have the confidence to speak their minds with a healthy dose of honor and respect. But what if we don't agree with them? I'll warn you now that even if you are very close with your adult children, chances are high that you won't always agree on everything. I'm not talking about anything unbiblical that goes against God's Word. It's all the other things in life on which we each have our own outlook, and that "we" includes our adult children too.

As my sons have grown, matured, and married, I've come to understand that we aren't always going to agree on every-thing. As long as we love and respect each other, though, we'll always land on love. My prayer and hope are that they continue to grow in their relationships with the Lord, their love with their wives, and their commitment to what God's Word says about life. Their hearts are no longer mine to hold—that honor belongs first to the Lord and second to their wives—but we are still connected by love.

Landing on love is the goal for our relationships with our adult children. In the grand scheme of life, our sons and daughters are under our care for only a short time. They do not belong to us—they belong to the Father. We are not one with our children, nor are we called to be. We are called to be one with our spouses. The beauty of a Christian family is that we are *all* one with the Father, and loving and serving Him is the common denominator that binds us together.

> **Landing on love is the goal for our relationships with our adult children.**

EVERYTHING WITH LOVE

Be on guard. Stand firm in the faith. Be courageous. Be strong. And do everything with love (1 Corinthians 16:13–14).

In this verse, the apostle Paul instructs us on how to live a Christ-filled life, and he tells us the way to do it at the end: "Do everything with love." *Love.* That's the key, isn't it? That's why God sent Jesus to die on the cross for our sins and be our Savior. Because He loves us!

As moms, our love for our families often shows through our actions. However, our children to need to hear it too. The following are some words and phrases we can use anytime, regardless of our children's ages, to speak our love:

- God loves you.
- I love you.
- I forgive you.
- I'm sorry.
- Please forgive me.
- Thank you.
- You're welcome.
- Way to go!
- I'm proud of you.
- I love you more.

"I love you more." I cannot tell you how many times I said that to my sons when they were young. They would reply, "I love *you* more." After going back and forth a couple of times, I would cheerfully tell them, "No, I love you more, because I'm your mother." That says it all. We love more because we're moms.

//////////

If I had to do it all over again, would I do anything differently? I would have trusted the Lord to guide my heart and direct my steps a lot sooner, and I would not have allowed myself to worry so much. You might be thinking, *Well, it's easy for you to say that now. Your children are all grown up!* Yes, they are adults, and yes, my role has changed significantly from when they were young. However, I still have to make the choice to trust the Lord and believe in His perfect plan for every member of my family.

My final word of encouragement to you is this: make it your daily goal to find joy. It's in the everyday moments of mother-hood where the lifelong memories are made. From the moments you hold your newborns, to the wet kisses from your toddlers, to the hugs from your children who are now taller than you are, to the moment you look into their eyes on their wedding days ... find the joy of being Mom and embrace the adventure.

> May our sons flourish in their youth
>> like well-nurtured plants.
> May our daughters be like graceful pillars,
>> carved to beautify a palace.
> May our barns be filled
>> with crops of every kind.
> May the flocks in our fields multiply by the thousands,
>> even tens of thousands,
>> and may our oxen be loaded down with produce.
> May there be no enemy breaking through our walls,
>> no going into captivity,
>> no cries of alarm in our town squares.
> Yes, joyful are those who live like this!
>> Joyful indeed are those whose God is the LORD
>> (Psalm 144:12–15).

CHAPTER 11

STUDY GUIDE

REVIEW

Every family has a legacy. A godly legacy is not one that is perfect but rather one that reflects the need for our Savior and brings Him honor and praise. Our stories are reminders of God's faithfulness. He loves us simply because we belong to Him, and when we realize this, we can face any parenting challenge with confidence. Our children are under our care for only a short time. The process of letting go can be emotional, but as their dependence on us decreases, we can find great joy in watching their dependence on God increase.

SCRIPTURES

- Psalm 78:1–8
- Psalm 145:1–7
- Proverbs 6:20–23
- Romans 15:13

QUESTIONS

- What intangible gifts do you hope to pass down as a legacy to future generations?
- How does recognizing God's unfailing love help you cope with the challenges of your current season of motherhood?
- Why do you think it is important for your children to hear you say, "I love you"?

HEART CONNECTORS

- Ask the Lord, "In addition to loving and serving You, what do You want my family to be known for?" Write down what He brings to your mind or shows you in His Word. Pray with your husband about these ideas. Decide on two or three action steps you can put into practice right now. Then share these steps with your children and begin to develop a godly legacy as a family.

- Write a letter to each of your children and tell them how happy you are to be their mom. Share some of the ways they bring you joy every day. Add a photograph of a sweet or fun memory and mail the letter. If you have adult children who are married, include their spouses in the letters and enclose pictures of their early days together.

PRAYER

Father God, thank You for the incredible opportunity I have to leave a lasting legacy for my children and for future generations. In 3 John 4, Your Word says, "I could have no greater joy than to hear that my children are following the truth." I pray that my children will follow You all the days of their lives. Thank You for Your love that gives me strength and hope. Because of You, I can find joy every day. May everything I do as a mom and as Your daughter bring You glory, honor, and praise. In Jesus' name, Amen.

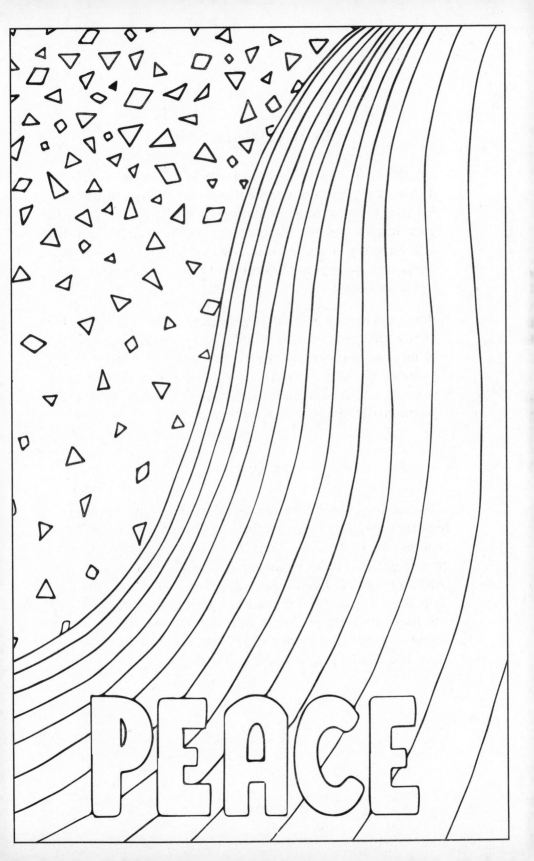

ABOUT THE AUTHOR

J udy and her husband, Mike, have been married more than 30 years. They attend Gateway Church in Southlake, Texas, where Mike is the Executive Pastor to the Senior Pastor. For more than a decade, Judy has enjoyed teaching and speaking on marriage, parenting, and all things Jesus! She has a bachelor's degree in Mass Communications from Pan American University (known today as The University of Texas Rio Grande Valley). Judy and Mike have two adult sons and two wonderful daughters-in-love. Jacob is married to Neeli, and Joel is married to Danielle (Danny).